INSTRUCTIONAL
LEADERSHIP
HOW PRINCIPALS MAKE A DIFFERENCE

Wilma F. Smith
Richard L. Andrews

Association for Supervision and Curriculum Development
Alexandria, Virginia

Wilma F. Smith is Superintendent of Schools, Mercer Island School District, Mercer Island, Washington.

Richard L. Andrews is Dean of the College of Education, University of Wyoming, Laramie.

Typeset by Scott Photographics, Inc.
Printed by Edwards Brothers, Inc.
ASCD Stock Number: 611-89142
ISBN: 0-87120-164-X
Price: $14.95

Library of Congress Cataloging-in-Publication Data

Smith, Wilma F.
  Instructional leadership : how principals make a difference /
Wilma F. Smith and Richard L. Andrews.
      p.   cm.
  Includes bibliographical references.
  ISBN 0-87120-164-X
  1. School principals.   2. Leadership.   I. Andrews, Richard L.
II. Title.
LB2831.9.S64   1989
371.2′012—dc20   89-37232
                                                              CIP

Instructional Leadership: How Principals Make A Difference

Foreword

A central theme in *Instructional Leadership: How Principals Make A Difference* is that educators have great moral, ethical, and legal obligations to create good schools—places where all children can achieve their full potential and receive an equal opportunity to succeed in society. Central to that goal, the authors assert, are principals who act as instructional leaders.

Most of us can easily describe strong, effective principals, but "the imagery seems to be more elusive when we describe the principal as a strong instructional leader." Using the literature, research, and case studies of principals in practice, Wilma Smith and Richard Andrews draw a clear portrait of the instructional leader that others can emulate.

From the perspectives of theory and practice, Smith and Andrews discuss four key qualities of instructional leaders: resource provider, instructional resource, communicator, and visible presence. They draw on research about principal behavior to show that strong instructional leaders spend a substantially greater percentage of time on educational program improvement. An important focus of the book is reflective practice, specifically reflection on the "core technology of schooling—teaching and learning. . . ."

The case studies in Chapter 4 show how principals with very different communication, management, and personal styles can all be strong instructional leaders. Next, the authors describe a supervision model that can help all principals become better instructional leaders. Consistent with current literature on organizational theory and practice, they emphasize the importance of the underlying themes and values that hold a system together.

The combination of theory and practice in *Instructional Leadership: How Principals Make A Difference* makes it an especially valuable guide for educators who want to foster instructional leadership in their schools. It also contributes directly to ASCD's mission of developing leadership for quality in education for all students.

PATRICIA C. CONRAN
ASCD PRESIDENT, 1989–90

Preface

The observations about effective school principals we present in this book are based on our experiences in schools as students, teachers, administrators, and teachers of teachers and administrators. Our model for improving professional practice of school principals has been developed from two streams of inquiry—reflection on what happens daily in practice and an academic quest for understanding based on ideals about what principals should do to improve the learning environment for children.

At the heart of our work are some fundamental notions about what school administrators are obliged to do in a compulsory system of schooling. Those of us who become educational leaders assume enormous obligations under a compulsory schooling system in a democratic society. The most important obligation is to build a structure of relationships within schools so that all children learn. To fulfill this obligation, the most important function of educational leadership is to create good schools. By creating good schools, we mean that principals and superintendents use their professional knowledge and skills to foster conditions where all children can grow to their full potential.

Much thought has been given to what makes a good school. To have a good school, we must attend to the quality of the workplace for teachers. This focus makes sense. Intuition alone suggests that teachers who feel that their environment enhances their ability to teach will perform at a higher level than will teachers who have negative feelings about their workplace. Thus, increasing the opportunity for quality teaching in each classroom is good, common sense. Doing so will allow us to create good schools, and creating good schools is what this book is all about.

Over the past several years, we have reviewed, listened to, and read what thousands of parents are saying about their children's schools. When these parents enroll their children in the public schools, they believe they're turning those children over to the state. And they trust the state. It makes little difference whether parents are rich or poor; black, white, Hispanic, Native American, or Asian; male or female; whether their children come from single-parent or dual-parent homes; whether they walk or drive their children to school or put them on a school bus; or whether they're even at home when their children leave for school—these parents believe that we will give their children equality of opportunity to succeed in our society. This trust is our obligation, and more: as professional educators we accept enormous ethical, moral, and legal responsibilities.

We agree with John Goodlad that teaching is a moral profession—that is, only good things, or the right things, should happen as a result of our behavior. It is thus the role of administrators to orchestrate the activities of teachers so that good things do indeed happen in schools.

We believe that the research started by Ron Edmonds in 1979, the effective schools movement, supports the conclusion that what principals and teachers do collectively on a day-to-day basis has a powerful influence over the behavior of individual teachers as they interact with children in their classrooms. And the role that principals play as they interact with teachers makes a profound impact on teacher behavior and student learning.

In this book we offer the view that the leadership of the school principal is critical to improving the workplace for teachers. We focus on constructing a definition of instructional leadership that is observable and measurable in the school. We began our research on the principalship with the assumption that teachers are the best judges of the effectiveness of the principal's instructional leadership. Using the literature and the perceptions of teachers, we created a definition of instructional leadership and then conducted behavioral analyses of what principals do, and we analyzed what we know about the validity of principal leadership and children's learning. Finally, we developed a school-based supervision and evaluation model that can be used by supervisors of school principals to assess principals as instructional leaders, help them understand their strengths and need for growth, and assist them in achieving those objectives. It can also be used as a peer coaching model for school principals whose supervisors have not implemented the model.

The contributions we found most helpful came from school principals who allowed us to study their behavior and helped us interpret the literature on principal behavior and find meaning in the enormous amount of data we gathered. We are grateful to over 1,200 school principals who allowed us to intrude on their lives and schools so that we could better understand the nature of instructional leadership. To our colleagues—Roger Soder, Jackie Hallett, Susan Torrens, Debbie Jean Wing, Jan Reeder, John Morefield, Louise McKinney, Bob Strode, Bob Estes, Helen McIntrye, Arland and Sandy Tangeman, and Dale Bolton, who have served in various capacities (subjects, students, critics, confidants, and mentors)—we are deeply grateful for your friendship. We are indebted to the Seattle School District for providing its schools as a laboratory in our early work, the Bellevue and Mercer Island School Districts, and the University of Washington for providing fertile grounds for our ideas to flourish.

WILMA F. SMITH
RICHARD L. ANDREWS

1

The Principal as Instructional Leader

The school principalship has been the subject of hundreds of studies over the past 30 years. The central role of the principal has been viewed, variously, as building manager, administrator, politician, change agent, boundary spanner, and instructional leader. Principal attributes and hypothesized correlates selected for investigation are in large part derived from value stances concerning the relative importance that the researchers assigned to these several roles. During the last decade, these stances have centered on the principal as instructional leader, accountable for the academic achievement of students. Taken collectively, the "effective schools" studies reflect the view that the direct responsibility for improving instruction and learning rests in the hands of the school principal. In attempts to isolate commonalities among in-school variables, this basic approach has been criticized for its emphasis on outlier schools. Studies of this type usually examine schools where achievement levels are high for all students or where achievement differences between subpopulations of students are minimal.

More recently, the emergence of career-ladder plans, teacher centers, and the recommendation of the Carnegie Task Force on Teaching as a Profession for "lead teachers" suggests there should be a diminution of the principal's role as instructional leader. Discussions of these efforts usually reflect a political orientation and a concern for authority and power, with either teachers or principals seen as appropriate leaders. For the most part, such discussions have not included consideration of achievement and other school outcome measures.

Research from a variety of fields suggests that professionals associate the conditions under which they work with job satisfaction. Professionals who express positive feelings about their working conditions also appear to be more productive workers. More recent school effectiveness research has used this finding to focus research efforts on teacher satisfaction with the workplace and student achievement. This body of research, while less voluminous than the earlier outlier effective schools research, has found a powerful association between teachers' satisfaction with their professional role as classroom teachers and incremental growth in student academic achievement. It has also found that teachers' perception of the school principal as an instructional leader is the most powerful determinant of teachers' satisfaction with their professional role.

Improving teacher perceptions of the principal as an instructional leader is essential to the reading and mathematics achievement of students, particularly among historically low-achieving students (Andrews, Soder, and Jacoby 1986; Andrews and Soder 1987; Lezotte and Pasalacqua 1978; Glasmaw 1979; AASA 1980). Studies of teachers' perceptions of the principal as an instructional leader suggest that many practicing principals *are* instructional leaders. These studies also suggest, however, that many more principals fail to exhibit day-to-day instructional leadership behavior. If we are to improve the quality of schools, we must improve the professional practice of school principals. To do so, it is crucial that we (1) understand the meaning of "instructional leadership"; (2) develop school administration programs designed to select and educate principals who can perform such roles; (3) help school districts develop selection processes that will identify new principals who have these capabilities; and (4) implement supervision, evaluation, and staff development models that will allow quality decisions to be made by school district officials concerning the performance of their current corps of principals.

At the heart of our work to improve the professional practice of school principals are some fundamental notions about what school administrators are obliged to do in a compulsory system of schooling. Those of us who become school principals assume enormous obligations. The most important of these is to build a structure of relationships within the school so that all children have the opportunity to learn. To fulfill this obligation, school principals must create *good* schools. By *good* schools we mean that we use our professional knowledge and skills to create conditions in which each child can grow to his or her full potential and all children are given equal opportunity to succeed in our society. When these conditions are present, there is a measurable increase in the academic performance of children and at the same time, over time, the differences between groups of children (low-income v. affluent, ethnic v. white students) are reduced.

Reflections on Professional Practice
of School Principals

The importance of professional practice to the function of society has been well documented. Schön (1983) reminds us that virtually all of society's business is conducted by professionals with special training to provide health care, operate businesses, adjudicate laws, manage cities, design and construct buildings, and teach children. We are faced with providing leaders who can orchestrate the talents of these professionals so that patients get well, goods are produced, people receive due process, and students learn. There are nagging questions about what kind of leadership is appropriate and whether that leadership is universal for all types of organizations.

Providing appropriate leadership is an idea as old as civilization itself. Socrates, Aristotle, Lao Tzu all puzzled with notions about leadership—its function, its meaning, its methods, its value. And recently there has been a loss of confidence in all forms of leadership—elected, corporate, civic, religious, and educational. Loss of confidence in school leadership has come from a perception that our schools lack quality, that leadership ability is low among school principals, and that school leaders are more concerned about personal gain than serving the needs of children or society. To renew public confidence in school leaders will require the retention, recruitment, training, selection, and evaluation of a corps of school principals who clearly understand the meaning of schooling in a democratic society, possess leadership ability, and perform their professional roles in such a manner that teachers will commit their considerable energy to create good schools.

Most accept the view that to have a good school we must create a quality workplace for teachers and increase the opportunity for quality teaching in each classroom. However, the way to create these conditions is the subject of much debate. We are troubled by those who argue that good schools will result if we simply restructure them or increase degree requirements for teachers or give teachers more control over the curriculum and their classrooms or turn schools over to teachers and parents to run. Powell, Farrar, and Cohen (1985) and Goodlad (1984) suggest that the average classroom and its teacher is an island unto itself, rarely intruded upon by a school administrator for evaluative or improvement purposes, and that is the way the average teacher in the average school wants it to be. If this is the current condition, what, then, leads us to believe that the education of all children in those schools would improve if we restructure schools so that we take more of our good teachers out of the

3

classroom, or simply turn more of the control of our schools over to teachers and parents?

A thoughtful and promising basis for us to understand how we might create more good schools comes from the work of Schön (1983). Schön's thesis is that in order for professionals to meet the challenges of their work, they need to depend less on what they learned in graduate school than what they have learned in practice. Thus, the problem is how to make graduate school or the training of principals for professional practice more relevant so that when they reflect in practice, the broader framework of theory and research are the basis of that reflection. Schön's work suggests three types of reflective practice: reflection *in* action, reflection *on* action, and reflection *while in* action. The first, *reflection in action*, exists when the professional reflects about the problem rather than acting impulsively. The second, *reflection on action*, exists when the professional thinks critically about something that she has already done. The third, *reflection while in action*, suggests a condition in which the professional is on "automatic pilot" with professional routines and engages in critical inquiry about other things.

To understand this third condition, imagine that you're driving a car on the highway when something suddenly appears in front of you. You immediately, and without conscious thought, maneuver the car to avoid the obstacle. You are startled by the fact that you were not aware of your driving but were deep in thought about more important matters. This is *reflection while in action*. Often, the professional is engaged in her professional work following well-established routines that are on automatic pilot while thinking about other matters. Thoughts about these other matters do not disrupt the professional's ability to perform or her subconscious thoughts about her professional work. Some of our colleagues believe that educational administrators *do not* engage in reflective practice. We suggest otherwise. The average school administrator does not fail to reflect, but simply reflects on lesser things than the purpose of schooling and curriculum and instruction issues.

To understand reflection on action, consider a debriefing session by a high school principal with the coaching staff and members of the faculty after a Friday night ballgame. The entire game can be replayed; critical moments can be recalled and views on strategy, good coaching, and athletes are easily brought into the analysis. Similarly, we want to turn the reflection of the school principal to the core technology of schooling— teaching and learning—and achieve the same level of reflection on curriculum, program development, and instruction that may well already go on with less important or critical matters. Daily routines that attend to the usual matters of schooling must be on automatic pilot, the unconscious guide to day-to-day behavior of school principals.

In the following sections, we offer some general notions about leader behavior and some underlying assumptions about why principals focus on managing the building rather than on instructional leadership issues. We conclude with a definition of instructional leadership based on work we conducted in over 200 schools with over 2,500 teachers and 1,200 school principals.

Competencies of Leadership

Bennis (1984) reminds us that there are four competencies of leaders—management of meaning, of attention, of trust, and self-management. To be competent as an educational leader, the individual must first be able to manage the meaning of schooling, which means that the leader has a clear understanding of the purpose for schools and can manage the symbols of the organization toward fulfilling that purpose—the primary theme about which all activity must be organized. Management of attention is the educational leader's ability to get teachers to focus and expand their energies toward fulfilling the purpose of school; e.g., they will use their talents to teach children. Management of trust means that leaders behave in such a way that others believe in them and their style of leadership does not become an issue. Management of self is simply, "I know who I am; I know my strengths and weaknesses. I play to my strengths and shore up my weaknesses."

Leadership, in the general sense, then, is necessarily constrained by the situations in which leadership is displayed. Over the past several years we have learned much about leadership in relation to organizational context and variables that might affect a leader's effectiveness in different situations. There has been far more research on the consequences of leader behavior than on the determinants of a leader's behavior. Our understanding of these circumstances has been constrained by a prevailing view that leaders shape organizations, not that organizations shape leaders.

Three theories have deepened our understanding of how conditions shape leader behavior: role, expectancy, and adaptive-reactive theory. Role theorists (Kahn and Rosenthal 1964, Pfeffer and Salancik 1975) suggest that the principal's leadership behavior is shaped by the perceptions of how other people (the superintendent, other principals, teachers, students, and parents) want the leader to behave. The principal's perception of role requirements is influenced by prescriptions such as job description, day-to-day requests, and orders and directions from the superintendent. Role expectations of teachers and students are communicated in a more subtle manner; a sensitive principal soon learns to recognize and respond to these role expectations. At times, various people make incompatible demands on the principal, creating "role conflicts" (Yukl 1981). In addition to these role expectations from other people, the principal's perception of role requirements depends on the nature of the school's mission and tasks. Role expectations for the principal are seldom concrete or comprehensive; he usually is able to shape his own role over time.

The second theory is expectancy theory (Nebecker and Mitchell 1974), which suggests that the principal's behavior can be predicted from her expectations about the consequences of the behavior. For example, if a principal perceives that keeping a neat, orderly building is more likely to win praise, she will keep a neat, orderly building. If not running a budget deficit brings praise, the principal will take great care in the administration of the school budget. Principals, in other words, choose courses of action that they perceive to have a high probability of obtaining the desired outcomes. A deficiency of using expectancy theory alone is that it does not explain how leaders formulate expectancies or why they value some outcomes more than others.

Finally, the adaptive-reactive school of thought of Osborn and Hunt (1975) suggests that principal behavior is a product of larger variables such as the structure of the school, centralized versus building-based decision making, the school's community and district, and the size of the school. The task at hand (e.g., scheduling students, monitoring the halls) and teacher attitudes and traits have some influence on how principals do their jobs. The type of school (high school, junior high or middle school, or elementary school), whether the school is large or small, and whether the school is in a stable or changing community would better predict the principal's behavior. The adaptive-reactive theory assumes that the principal *adapts* to the structure, size, and external environment variables and *reacts* to teacher attitudes and traits.

When any of these theories are used singly, research seems to provide only modest support for predictions of principal behavior. Taken collectively, however, the theories seem to provide a good foundation for explaining and changing principal behavior. If we want principals to be instructional leaders, we must develop job descriptions that are compatible with fulfilling such a role, evaluate the performance of the principal on these job dimensions, educate teachers and parents on the value of such roles, and buffer the school from environmental or community forces that would press for a different kind of principal behavior. There are numerous characteristics and associated behaviors and activities that must be planned for and implemented if principals are to be instructional leaders.

Characteristics and Behaviors
of Instructional Leaders

Observation, common sense, and intuition help us formulate an image of a good principal, a strong principal, an effective principal. Such principals are often referred to in glowing terms: "runs a tight ship," "sure keeps the parents at bay," "knows the district inside and out," or "keeps the building ship-shape." However, the imagery seems to be more elusive when we describe the principal as a strong instructional leader.

Defining strong leadership is not a modern problem. Biographers, historians, social scientists, and educational researchers have discussed the concept of leadership for decades. Bennis (1984, Bennis and Nanus 1985) notes that there are more than 350 definitions of leadership recorded in the literature. Those definitions include Bennis and Nanus' (1985) suggestion that strong leaders are able to involve everyone in pursuing a shared mission. Thomson (AASA 1983, p. 19) defines leadership as "getting the job done through people." Schmuck (1985), using the work of McGregor, defines leadership as "inducing followers to act toward goals that represent the values of both the leaders and the followers."

Various theories have been offered to explain what leaders do, how they behave, what attributes they possess, and how varying situations affect styles of leadership (Andrews 1985; McCormack-Larkin 1985; Miller 1985; Hallenger and Murphy 1985; Goodlad 1984; Dwyer 1984; Cawelti 1984; Purkey and Smith 1982; Edmonds 1979, 1982; Leithwood and Montgomery 1982; Wilson 1982; Liphan 1981; Bossert, Dwyer, Rowan, and Lee 1981; Roe and Drake 1980; Wynne 1980; Rutter, Maughan, Mortimore, Outson, and Smith 1979; Brookover 1977). How we define leadership of the school principal seems to determine the extent to which it is a key element in producing an instructionally effective school.

Several distinctions between more effective and less effective principals have consistently emerged from the educational research. For example, Rutherford (1985, p. 32) notes that effective principals:

> (1) have clear, informed visions of what they want their schools to become—visions that focus on students and their needs; (2) translate these visions into goals for their schools and expectations for their teachers, students and administrators; (3) continuously monitor progress; and (4) intervene in a supportive or corrective manner when this seems necessary.

Persell and Cookson (1982, p. 22), who reviewed more than 75 research studies, report recurrent behaviors that seem to be associated with strong principals: (1) demonstrating a commitment to academic goals, (2) creating a climate of high expectations, (3) functioning as an instruc-

7

tional leader, (4) being a forceful and dynamic leader, (5) consulting effectively with others, (6) creating order and discipline, (7) marshaling resources, (8) using time well, and (9) evaluating results.

Taken collectively, these lists of characteristics suggest that the principal who is a strong leader functions as a forceful and dynamic professional through a variety of personal characteristics, including high energy, assertiveness, ability to assume the initiative, openness to new ideas, tolerance for ambiguity, a sense of humor, analytic ability, and a practical stance toward life. The principal who displays strong instructional leadership:

1. Places priority on curriculum and instruction issues.

2. Is dedicated to the goals of the school and the school district.

3. Is able to rally and mobilize resources to accomplish the goals of the district and the school.

4. Creates a climate of high expectations in the school, characterized by a tone of respect for teachers, students, parents, and community.

5. Functions as a leader with direct involvement in instructional policy by:
    a. communicating with teachers,
    b. supporting and participating in staff development activities,
    c. establishing teaching incentives for the use of new instructional strategies, and
    d. displaying knowledge of district-adopted curriculum materials.

6. Continually monitors student progress toward school achievement and teacher effectiveness in meeting those goals. Teacher evaluation is:
    a. characterized by frequent classroom visitation, clear evaluation criteria, and feedback, and
    b. is used to help students and teachers improve performance.

7. Demonstrates commitment to academic goals, shown by the ability to develop and articulate a clear vision of long-term goals for the school, and to strong achievement goals that are consistent with district goals and priorities.

8. Effectively consults with others by involving the faculty and other groups in school decision processes.
    a. Teachers feel they are genuinely encouraged to exchange ideas.
    b. Effectively functioning coalitions support the operation of the school, and constituent groups share a commitment to the academic mission of the school.
    c. A critical constructive force in the school encourages inquiry and change.

9. Effectively and efficiently mobilizes resources such as materials, time, and support to enable the school and its personnel to most effectively meet academic goals.

10. Recognizes time as a scarce resource and creates order and discipline by minimizing factors that may disrupt the learning process.

In their analyses of student achievement outcomes, Andrews and others found that when these behavioral descriptors were used to group schools in which teachers perceived their principals to be strong, average, or weak instructional leaders, there were significant differences in incremental growth in student academic achievement (Andrews and Soder 1985, 1987a, 1987b; Andrews, Houston, and Soder 1985; Andrews, Soder, and Jacoby 1986). Schools operated by principals who were perceived by their teachers to be strong instructional leaders exhibited significantly greater gain scores in achievement in reading and mathematics than did schools operated by average and weak instructional leaders. These general descriptors can be organized into four broad areas of strategic interaction between the school principal and teachers: (1) the principal as resource provider, (2) the principal as instructional resource, (3) the principal as communicator, and (4) the principal as visible presence.

The Principal as Resource Provider

As resource provider, the principal marshals personal, building, district, and community resources to achieve the vision and goals of the school. Personnel in the school are assigned with careful consideration for their strengths in content and personal skills. Personnel outside of the school are drawn in to help staff solve instructional problems and capitalize on opportunities. Materials appropriate for the curriculum are provided through skillful management of the instructional budget, with opportunity for staff input into the budgetary processes. The entire budget process is viewed as a professional activity that enables the school staff to maximize scarce resources and to set priorities for expenditures. Information is power, and the instructional leader shares data that enable staff members to participate knowledgeably in the decision-making processes. The principal uses group processes to get the most appropriate expertise and to make certain that up-to-date information flows through the school. Opportunities for new resources are sought by the principal—grants, workshops, professional conferences, inservice training, college courses, and volunteer services. All are examined in terms of their value to the school's goals and priorities.

The principal as resource provider is well supported in the literature. For example, Persell (1982) found that successful principals are good at acquiring needed materials. One leader who was particularly successful in implementing Public Law 94-142 was "unusually adept at getting what he desired from the higher levels of the school system, and was able to bring this talent into the service of children with special needs." Success at procuring needed materials may be due to both administrative skills and school district conditions. Restraints may be set by legal conditions, collective bargaining agreements, past events, or a variety of other factors. However, individuals can act in quite different ways to the same set of conditions. The range of individual practices among the principals in any given system is wide, and a major factor that explains that variation is how individual principals conceive of the system (Sarason 1971, p. 140, 1982).

Routine administrative tasks—discipline, providing an orderly school climate, personnel management, facilities management, and budget—are all a part of mobilizing resources. The importance of the managerial aspects should not be minimized. The effective principal, nevertheless, seems to be able to blend and balance these elements through time management. Certainly the size of the school, the experience of the staff, and the support and priorities of the central office may all be variables that have some impact on the principal's ability to blend and balance the behaviors associated with strong leadership. The point here is not to detail what the effective schools research says about orderly, purposeful climate or what leadership and managerial research says about the best way to prepare a budget, select a teacher, delegate responsibility, or manage time. It is, however, important for the strong instructional leader to be able to analyze and understand the resources that need to be managed.

Educational organizations are best described as "loosely coupled" rather than as tightly connected and controlled (Weick 1982). Weick notes that one reason some schools may be ineffective is that they are managed with the wrong theory in mind. According to Weick, we assume that schools are self-correcting organizations staffed by people who are interdependent, have consensus on goals, and have predictable problems and solutions. He notes that, in fact, none of these characteristics is true of schools and how they function. Effective school administrators in "loosely coupled" schools need to take advantage of symbol management to tie the system together. He further notes:

> People need to be part of sensible projects. Their action becomes richer, more confident and more satisfying when it is linked with important underlying themes, values and movement. . . . Administrators must be attentive to the "glue" that holds loosely coupled systems together because such forms are just barely systems (1982, p. 675).

Weick also reminds us that:

the administrator who manages symbols does not just sit in his or her office mouthing clever slogans. Eloquence must be disseminated. And since channels are unpredictable, administrators must get out of their office and spend lots of time one-on-one—both to remind people of central visions and to assist them in applying these visions to their own activities. The administrator teaches people to interpret what they are doing in a common language (1982, p. 676).

Sergiovanni (1984) contends that schools are both tightly and loosely coupled. Using the work of Peters and Waterman on the best-run corporations, Sergiovanni notes that excellent schools have a clear sense of purpose and structure, yet at the same time a great deal of freedom is allowed for staff and students to determine how the purpose is to be realized. This combination of a tight and loose structure, Sergiovanni asserts, gives meaning and control and allows people to experience success.

Thus, managing the daily operation of a school is a complex task in a complex organizational environment. A strong leader recognizes that management of resources cannot be addressed by simple formulas or by emphasizing one element of leadership at the expense of others.

In essence, strong instructional leaders have the capacity to mobilize available resources to implement policies that lead to desired outcomes. To mobilize other resources, a principal must have a good grasp of what is possible and the ability to convince potentially competing groups to work together. Effective leaders intuitively apply the theories that present leadership as systems of individuals and resources and that recognize appropriate substitutes for leadership (Manasse 1984).

Effective principals view resource provision in terms of maximizing instructional effectiveness and student achievement. They view resource provision as much more than money or supplies—as encouragement of human resources that help the faculty and students achieve success. Effective principals have the capacity and energy to closely monitor all aspects of the school program—teaching, learning, and the environment. Strong instructional leaders have the ability to analyze and manage resources in a way that allows the entire school community to realize its potential.

The success of the principal to mobilize resources is reflected in the following ways.

The Principal as Resource Provider

1. The instructional leader demonstrates effective use of time and resources.

    a. Plans, organizes, schedules, and prioritizes work to be done.

    b. Delegates work as appropriate.

  c. Assigns staff members according to their strengths.

2. The instructional leader demonstrates skill as a change master by establishing an ongoing process for planning and making necessary changes within the school while developing a feeling of individual/group ownership.

  a. Creates a positive climate for change and nurtures creative approaches to change.

  b. Uses skills needed to manage change.

  c. Evaluates the effectiveness of change.

3. The instructional leader demonstrates the ability to motivate staff members.

  a. States clear expectations to the staff.

  b. Provides clear feedback.

  c. Encourages the staff to take risks and to innovate.

4. The instructional leader knows staff members' strengths and weakness and knows about instructional resources that may be helpful to them.

  a. Matches staff members' needs to staff development opportunities.

  b. Knows about resources that enhance instruction.

  c. Mobilizes resources and district support to help achieve academic goals.

  d. Convinces staff members that they are important instructional resource people in the school.

The Principal as Instructional Resource

  As instructional resource, the principal is actively engaged in the improvement of classroom circumstances that enhance learning. Through ongoing dialogue with the staff, the principal encourages the use of a variety of instructional materials and teaching strategies. The principal is sought out by teachers who have instructional concerns or innovative ideas. Clinical supervision complements teacher evaluation, with emphasis on continuing professional growth and development for everyone on the staff, including the principal. The principal and the staff consider evaluation, the highest level of cognition, to be cyclical. The most obvious role of the principal as an instructional resource is to facilitate good teaching.

  To facilitate good teaching, the principal must stay abreast of new developments in materials and strategies for improving instruction. The principal maintains a personal development program that includes regular review of educational research, curriculum development, and new advances in understanding how children learn.

  The most consistent finding in the majority of studies of school effectiveness is the crucial connection between expectation and achievement.

These studies seem to say that teachers and students live up to our expectations for them (Brookover and Lezotte 1977, Persell and Cookson 1982, Edmonds 1979, Rutter et al. 1979). Successful schools result when goals are clear, reasonable, uniform, and perceived as important, and when the staff is committed to them. In these and similar studies, researchers consistently emphasize the principal's important role in establishing the vision, expectations, and commitment to goals. The important point is that more effective schools have a shared vision, and a strong instructional leader is responsible for establishing and communicating that vision.

The principal must attend to differences in staff members' attitudes about student ability to learn (Austin 1979, Edmonds 1979, Frederickson and Edmonds 1979) and to the feelings of both teachers and students that what they do makes a difference (Sergiovanni 1984). According to Gauthier (1980, pp. 16-17), "every school must believe that all children can learn and that all teachers and administrators can help them."

Effective principals seem to differ significantly from less effective principals in the way they interpret and implement the concept of a good school environment. Effective principals seem to be able to allocate building resources in ways that maximize teacher effectiveness and student achievement. In addition, they selectively and systematically apply other support mechanisms such as advantageous scheduling, careful assignment of teachers, and the dispensing of recognition to achieve these ends. The more effective principals provide not only specific details about their teachers' performance but also insights into why teachers perform as they do (Rutherford 1985). Principals play a significant role in monitoring individual teachers' work and helping teachers master changes in classroom practice that will improve student outcomes.

The effective principal is actively involved in all aspects of the instructional program, sets expectations for continuous improvement and collegiality, models the kinds of behaviors desired, participates in inservice training with teachers, and consistently gives priority to instructional concerns.

The role of instructional resource requires the principal to be knowledgeable about teaching. Sapone (1985) maintains that any school can increase efficiency and effectiveness if the principal is able to demonstrate curriculum and instructional leadership. She suggests that the model used makes little difference; what is important is consistency in the use of a total curriculum plan/model as developed and implemented within the school and as advocated and endorsed by the staff and the school principal. In other words, the principal must ensure that teachers have a well-designed curricular program and that meaningful teaching is critical to that design. Similarly, Lipham (1981) suggests that the improvement of teaching and learning is the foremost function of the principal. He concludes that principals must do more than just "know about" the instructional program; they must be "intimately involved in its development, implementation, evaluation, and refinement." In exemplary schools, the principal shows strong knowledge of and participation in instructional activities (Austin 1979, Fullan 1981).

Although a principal may not have specific knowledge of every curricular area taught in the school, his knowledge should at least embrace the general trends in each subject area. The effective principal must have sufficient knowledge to understand and evaluate curricular innovations and be familiar with effective teaching methods and the principles of learning. When principals know the basics of learning and instruction, they can help teachers improve, regardless of the subject matter.

The Principal as Instructional Resource

1. The instructional leader demonstrates the ability to evaluate and reinforce appropriate and effective instructional strategies.

   a. Knows and shares the latest research findings on teaching and learning with the staff so new ideas are tried.

   b. Expresses knowledge of effective strategies for students in different age groups.

   c. Uses knowledge and skill in effective instructional strategies.

2. The instructional leader supervises the staff, using strategies that focus on the improvement of instruction.

   a. Documents instructional performance of teachers.

   b. Conducts post-conferences that include developmental objectives suggested by the staff member or administrator.

   c. Provides staff members with evidence of continuity between clinical supervision observations.

3. In the process of assessing the educational program, the instructional leader uses student outcome information that is directly related to instructional issues.

   a. Reads and interprets district standardized and criterion-referenced test information.

   b. Develops intervention procedures designed to identify strengths and remediate weaknesses.

   c. Identifies uses of external consultant evaluation assistance where needed.

4. The instructional leader demonstrates successful application of the district's personnel evaluation policies.

a. Designs appropriate annual evaluation cycles to include effective goal setting with the employee and appropriate measurement of these goals.

b. Conferences effectively with employees regarding performance.

5. The instructional leader knows the importance of student learning objectives to the implementation of the instructional program.

a. Communicates to staff and community the extent to which learning objectives for the school have been mastered.

b. Assists teachers in the mastery of student learning objectives.

The Principal as Communicator

As communicator, the principal articulates a vision of the school that heads everyone in the same direction. The principal's day-to-day behavior communicates that she has a firm understanding of the purpose of schooling and can translate that meaning into programs and activities within the school.

Effective communication must be displayed at three levels—one-to-one, small group, and large group—to articulate the vision of the school to the school district, parents, and the larger community. The principal as communicator has mastered confrontation and active listening skills, can facilitate the work of leaderless groups, and understands how to communicate school direction to outside forces that would move the school away from the direction the staff and principal have chosen.

The principal uses communication as the basis for developing sound relationships with staff through behavior that is consistent, objective, and fair. The principal communicates so that both the content and processes for communication are explicit. What topics, for example, may be discussed openly by the entire staff, by parent-staff councils, by students and staff, or by supervisor-teacher dyads? What structures and processes will be used by what groups to make which decisions about the governance of the school? How much autonomy does the staff have in the decision-making processes? Which decisions will be made by the principal with the advice and counsel of the staff? How do building decisions fit into the scheme of the school district's processes? All of these questions must be answered through the principal's leadership and communication with the staff. Communication processes are important. The principal makes a commitment to those processes in establishing school goals, together with the staff, parents, and students. Resources are committed to the goals, and evaluation systems are established. Frequent reference is made to goals, and classroom observations, inservice topics, and faculty meetings focus on those priorities.

How instructional leaders identify and communicate a vision for the school varies, based on the principal's style of leadership (Andrews, Soder, and Jacoby 1986; Andrews 1986, 1988; Andrews and Soder 1987a, 1987b; Esther 1985). The salient message is that the strong principal has a vision and is able to clearly articulate that vision. Communication of vision is perhaps the most important way for a principal to exert effective leadership—to leave no doubt about school priorities. Sergiovanni (1984) describes communication of vision as "purposing." Purposing is the process of emphasizing selective attention and modeling important goals and behaviors in such a manner that it signals others of what is valued in the school.

Principals as leaders of high-performing systems focus their organization on well-defined, basic purposes. Their leadership is directed toward creating a commitment to purpose. They are aware of the value of symbolic actions and the influence of culture on productive organizational climates. Effective principals have a vision of their schools and of their role in making the vision become a reality. Vail (1982) incorporates the "vision" in his concept of purposing as a continuous stream of actions by an organization's formal leadership that has the effect of fostering clarity, consensus, and commitment for the organization's basic purposes. Vail found that leaders of high-performing systems have strong feelings about the attainment of purposes, focus on issues and variables, and put in extraordinary amounts of time to achieve their purposes.

Principals in effective schools consistently demonstrate a commitment to academic goals. They are able to develop and articulate a vision of instructional goals that prioritize school and classroom activities (Bamburg and Andrews 1988). Most important, this vision brings coherence and integration to instructional planning by the school staff. The ways in which vision is used to provide instructional leadership are documented in a number of studies. For example, goals are used to clarify expectations for program implementation (Dow and Whitehead 1980, Gross, Giaquinta, and Bernstein 1971). Effective principals use goals to provide a focus for communication, conveying support of the enthusiasm for goal-related work and for conveying school needs to district administrators (Blumberg and Greenfield 1980, Reinhardt, Arends, Burns, Kutz, and Wyant 1979). The vision established by the instructional leader and the process for the development of vision helps provide a climate of high expectations and mutual respect among staff members and students (Persell and Cookson, 1982).

Leaders typically express symbolic aspects of leadership by searching beneath the surface of events and activities for deeper meaning and value. These leaders bring to the school a sense of drama that permits people to rise above the daily routine. They are able to see the significance of what a group is doing and could be doing. They urge people to go beyond the routine—to break out of the mold into something more lively and vibrant. Finally, symbolic leaders are able to communicate their sense of vision by words and examples. They use easily understood language symbols that communicate a sense of purpose so that everyone shares ownership of the school. Vision becomes the substance of what is communicated as symbolic aspects of leadership are emphasized (Sergiovanni 1984).

The literature suggests that effective principals have a clear vision of goals and are strongly oriented to those goals (Rosenblum and Jastrzab 1975). This vision is reflected in the principals' long-term goals and visions for their schools and teachers (Hall, Rutherford, Hord, and Huling 1984). Clear vision seems to allow school principals to organize the school activities so that they are not continually putting out "brush fires" (Blumberg and Greenfield in Fullan 1981). Sergiovanni (1984) has described the role of the principal in communicating the vision of the school as the "high priest"—one who seeks to define, strengthen, and articulate those enduring values, beliefs, and cultural strands that give the school its identity. The net effect of vision communication is to bond students, staff members, parents, and the community as believers in the work of the school.

Teachers perceive that communication with principals who are strong instructional leaders results in improved instructional practice in their classrooms, helps them to understand that the relationship between instructional practices and student achievement provides a basis for clearly understanding evaluative criteria, and establishes a clear sense of the direction of the school (Andrews and Soder 1987, Andrews, Soder, and Jacoby 1985).

The success of the principal as a good communicator is reflected in the following dimensions of the instructional leadership role.

The Principal as Communicator

1. The instructional leader demonstrates the ability to evaluate and deal effectively with others.

   a. Engages in two-way communication accurately, sensitively, and reliably.

   b. Promotes mutual conflict resolution, problem solving, cooperation, and sharing.

   c. Recognizes what information is appropriate to communicate.

2. The instructional leader speaks and writes clearly and concisely.

   a. Displays good organization skills in oral and written communication.

   b. Demonstrates coherence in oral and written communication.

c. Recognizes needs and interacts appropriately with specific audiences in the educational community.

3. The instructional leader applies skills and strategies of conflict management that satisfy the interest of both parties in a practical and acceptable manner.

a. Sees others' points of view and clearly articulates them in conflict situations.

b. Displays the ability to help others arrive at mutually acceptable solutions.

c. Manages conflict effectively.

4. The instructional leader facilitates groups in selecting courses of action through problem-solving techniques.

a. Identifies and collects valid, relevant, and reliable information to accurately assess the current situation.

b. Develops and analyzes solutions to complex problems.

c. Develops an implementation plan that includes provisions for evaluation.

5. The instructional leader demonstrates the ability to use a variety of group process skills in interaction with the staff, parents, and students.

a. Helps others to develop a commitment to a process for goal achievement.

b. Assists in formulating the final outcome in a way that can be clearly understood and applied.

c. Develops and implements procedures for evaluating both process and outcome.

6. The instructional leader demonstrates skill in working as a team member.

a. Assesses strengths and weakness of team members.

b. Demonstrates strong group process skills.

c. Demonstrates the ability to integrate group and personal goals.

The Principal as Visible Presence

As a visible presence, the principal interacts with Staff and students in classrooms and hallways, attends grade-level and departmental meetings, and strikes up spontaneous conversations with teachers. The principal's presence is felt throughout the school as the keeper of the vision. The visible principal constantly displays behavior that reinforces school values. The principal knows on a first-hand basis what is going on daily in the school. The principal demonstrates these values as he protects the school from others' special interests. The presence of the principal is felt in formal and informal observations of classroom teachers. After being out and around the school, the principal communicates praise verbally and through informal written notes.

The visible presence of the principal appears to be most keenly felt when the principal serves as rewarder, giving positive attention to staff and student accomplishments. Brookover and his associates (1982) suggest that setting up an award system that clearly "strokes" staff and students for academic success is perhaps the most important aspect of creating an effective school. Acknowledging the achievements of others is a regular practice by principals who are strong instructional leaders (Giammetteo 1981). Being positive, cheerful, and encouraging; making themselves accessible to the staff, making their presence felt often by moving around the building; doing things with teachers; and involving teachers and getting the staff to express and set their own goals are overlapping elements of positive school climates and effective, visible principals (Iannaccone and Jamgochian 1985).

In high-achieving schools, principals emphasize instruction as the most important goal (Brookover and Lezotte 1977). One indicator of consensus on commitment to the goals of academic achievement is reflected in the way principals expect teachers to give their personal time. In the schools with higher achievement, teachers are willing to do this, but in those with lower achievement, teachers are not willing to give extra time unless they are paid for it. One way that principals are able to get greater teacher commitment is by being role models themselves. If the principal puts in long hours, is fair-minded in dealing with student complaints, and attends student activities in the school and the community, a positive tone is set for both teachers and students.

Effective elementary school principals express dissatisfaction with their day if their presence is not felt in every classroom every day. Middle/junior high and high school principals feel their week is not successful unless their presence is felt in every classroom once a week.

Teachers perceive their principal to be a visible presence if she makes frequent classroom observations, is accessible to discuss matters dealing with instruction, is regularly seen in and about the building, and actively participates in staff development activities.

The Principal as a Visible Presence

1. The instructional leader works cooperatively with the staff and the community to develop clear goals that relate to the district's mission.

    a. Expresses a clear vision for the school.

    b. Organizes people and resources to accomplish building and district goals.

2. The instructional leader is visible to the staff, students, and parents at the school.

a. Drops into classrooms informally without disrupting the instruction process.

b. Displays behavior consistent with the articulated vision for the school.

c. Defers other matters and actively participates in staff development activities.

d. Buffers the school from the external environment.

e. Manages time to be "out and around" during school hours.

f. Makes it possible for others to express an understanding of the principal's commitment to the priority goals of the school.

g. Communicates clearly the obligations of educators for student learning.

2

Performing the Role

The principal's role in delivering quality education has long been recognized as an important organizational characteristic of schools. How principals should perform their roles, however, has been the subject of debate. The profession has struggled with whether the principal is an instructional leader or a building manager, a member of a school family of professional educators or a mid-level management representative of the central administration.

The resolution of these issues has important implications for the representation of administrators' professional interests, the nature of administrator training programs, the general image of the principal in the local community, and the principal's day-to-day working conditions. The management or administrative-team concept suggests a need for a single, unified professional organization, a generic type of training program, single certification programs, common job descriptions, and equal pay. On the other hand, a view of the principal as a highly specialized professional with a role related to the size, location, and type of school (high school, middle/junior high, or elementary) suggests a need for a multiple-role organizational structure, role-specific training programs, multiple certification standards, and specialized job descriptions.

The lack of resolution of these issues has resulted in a dual structure for representing administrators' professional interests at the national and state levels. Similarly, there is confusion in the nature of programs for preservice training and staff development for school administrators. Central to this debate is whether there are basic and fundamental differences between or among elementary, middle/junior high, and high school principals. Further, there are questions about basic and fundamental differences between or among principals in large or small and urban, suburban, or rural schools.

In an effort to shed light on these issues, Andrews and Hallett (1983) conducted a study with a sample of 1,006 principals in the state of Washington. The results of this study seem to support the underlying assumption that while elementary, middle/junior high, and senior high school principals administer programs that serve different populations of students and have different structures and programs, the principals are substantially alike in the importance, ideal frequency, and actual time they designate to the various aspects of their jobs. Of the variables identified in the Andrews and Hallett study, however, the type of school administered accounted for the greatest variation in the principals' perceptions of the time required to do the job and how they actually spent their time. Several other variables seem to account, albeit to a lesser extent, for perceptual variations. These factors were size of school, size of district, type of district, and gender of the principal.

The specific conclusions from this study include:

1. Principals in elementary, middle/junior high, and senior high schools *do not* hold different values about what is important in the principal's job, nor do they hold different views about how they should ideally spend their time.

2. Principals in different-sized districts (large, medium, small) or different-sized schools *do not* hold different values about what is important in their jobs, nor do they hold different views about how they ideally should spend their time.

3. Principals in elementary, middle/junior high, and senior high schools hold different opinions about how much total time it takes them to do their jobs on a day-to-day basis. High school principals perceive that they need to spend more time to get the job done than do their elementary counterparts.

4. The analysis of actual time spent at their jobs confirms that high school and middle school principals spend more hours at their jobs than do their elementary counterparts, and these additional hours are devoted to supervising students and managing the school.

5. Size of school district and size of school have some bearing on how principals spend their time. Principals in large and very small school districts tend to spend less time on supervision of students than do their counterparts in medium-size school districts. And principals in large school districts tend to spend more time on coordination with external agencies than do principals in medium- and small-sized school districts.

6. Size of school also relates to the ability of principals to spend their

time on activities that they perceive to be most important. The larger the school, the more time the principal devotes to community relations and the more total time the principal spends on the job.

Thus, the differences found by Andrews and Hallett tended to be among those activities that principals perceive as least important in their jobs—operations and building management activities. While these differences are in the least important parts of the job, we must not lose sight of them as we work toward transforming principals' behavior from a building management focus to an instructional leader focus.

The Principal as Instructional Leader

The role of the principal is by no means a simple one. Thus, identifying factors that influence how principals perform their professional roles is equally complex. To gain insights into how or why principals perform as they do, we need to know what parts of the job principals typically consider to be most important and how they perceive they ideally should spend their time as they perform that role. Then we need to contrast this with how the average principal actually spends time and how this differs from principals who perform the role with a focus on instructional leadership activities. Understanding these issues will allow us to design training activities to help school principals improve their instructional leadership skills.

As used here, *principal as instructional leader* means that the principal is perceived by close associates as (1) providing the necessary resources so that the school's academic goals can be achieved; (2) possessing knowledge and skill in curriculum and instructional matters so that teachers perceive that their interaction with the principal leads to improved instructional practice; (3) being a skilled communicator in one-on-one, small-group, and large-group settings; and (4) being a visionary who is out and around creating a visible presence for the staff, students, and parents at both the physical and philosophical levels concerning what the school is all about.

The Values of the Average Principal

In our examination of the average principal, two issues are of primary importance—the value that principals place on the various dimensions of their roles and how they allocate time to those various dimensions. We need to understand the *values* of average school principals and then examine how they codify these values into their daily routines of running a school.

There have been two types of studies concerned with the importance principals attach to the various aspects of their jobs: those that have focused on general role orientation and those that have focused on the individual tasks or dimensions of the job. We focus here on a subset of both types of studies—specifically, those concerning perceptions of the principal performing a building management role versus an educational leadership role.

Those who have examined the role of the principal as building manager versus instructional leader suggest that the overall role orientation is related to the way principals perceive their time commitments and the way they actually spend their time. If we conceive of those activities that the principal engages in to maintain the current operations of the school to be building management, and those things that the principal must do to improve the learning environment for children to be instructional leadership activities, we can see a clearer picture of the interactive nature of these roles. The building management functions provide the foundation for the operation of the instructional program. And the degree to which the instructional program is effective affects the building management functions of the job. Thus, while we might separate the role into these two domains, we must not lose sight of the fact that there is everyday interaction between building management and instructional leadership. Clearly, also, the myriad tasks that make up the job must get done. It is not that some tasks can be set aside; rather, the issue concerns importance and value and how the principal allocates discretionary time to the various tasks that must be done.

Why do principals attach importance to certain dimensions of their jobs, and why do they feel that they have difficulty being instructional leaders? Interviews with principals suggest that three general barriers prevent principals from doing the instructional leadership parts of the job: (1) those related to the organizational context of schools, (2) those related to a set of professional norms, and (3) those related to the principal's lack of skills and district expectations.

As a group, principals say they lack time for supervision of instruction because they do not have adequate secretarial assistance or support staff to handle routine duties. Principals feel there is an imbalance in the allocation of authority and responsibility between the central office of the school district and the individual buildings. Too little of the authority for operating the building is delegated to principals; however, principals sense that they are held responsible for running a good school. Others express feelings that the day-to-day needs of the school are so demanding that there simply are not enough hours left in the day for instructional leadership activities. Other principals say that their hands are tied when they try to bring about changes in staff and programs because of collective bargaining agreements. The nature of policy making and the administration of policy from the district level often makes principals feel unsure of what actions they should or may take. They also express frustrations about expectations for the performance of instructional leadership activities when their university program trained them to be building managers. Finally, their school districts seem to expect them to be instructional leaders but reward them for well-managed, efficiently operated schools.

While these studies provide some insights about principals' perceptions of barriers to their work, they do not help us isolate the essential differences between those who are instructional leaders and those who are not. To understand these differences, we must examine the relative importance of the various tasks or dimensions of the principal's job and the behavior of principals as they go about running their schools.

What Do Principals Value?

It is not enough to say to a principal, "Go forth and orient yourself in such a way that you are an instructional leader." If we are to fashion programs to help principals perform instructional leadership activities and to produce future generations of school principals who can perform these functions, we must ask several questions. The first question is one of values: What do principals value most about their jobs? This question is important; if principals do not value instructional leadership activities, then changing their behavior will be difficult. The research on changing adult values is not encouraging. Deep-seated beliefs about what we should do are simply not easily changed. On the other hand, if principals value the instructional leadership part of their job more highly than they do the maintenance functions, then our task is to change their behavior to be consistent with their attitudes and values. The research on changing behavior provides much more promise for successful outcomes than does the research on changing attitudes and values. However, we should not delude ourselves into believing that changing adult behavior is easy.

Consider what we know about principals' values in relation to the various aspects of their jobs. Some of the research has focused exclusively on the actual way principals spend their time; most studies, however, have combined the analysis of how principals *think* they should spend their time with how they actually spend their time. The earliest of these types of studies was conducted by Krajewski in 1978 to determine what, if any, discrepancy exists between the roles principals play and the roles they prefer. The findings from this study resulted in two rankings: one, of the ideals (values) of school principals, and the other, of their actual daily performance. Krajewski found that principals placed the highest value on instructional leadership activities—supervision of instruction, curriculum development, and staff development—and the lowest value on management functions—community relations, discipline, and other pupil services. However, these same principals spent less time on instructional improvement activities than they did on routine management functions. There was a discrepancy between what the principals thought should receive their time and attention and how they *actually* spent their time.

The National Association of Secondary School Principals conducted a similar study in 1978. While their findings were not as dramatic as Krajewski's, they also showed discrepancies between how principals perceived their jobs and how they actually spent their time. School management was considered less important than program development, but it received far more of the principals' time and attention.

The Lake Washington School District, Kirkland, Washington (LWSD 1980), conducted an early effort to set forth expectations for changing principals from focusing on school management to improving instruction. In 1979, the district formed a task force to define the tasks of building administrators and started by conducting a two-week time-utilization study. Administrators were asked to "identify the percentage of time that should be devoted to each of their job dimensions" and to keep a log of the actual time they spent performing the tasks in each dimension. This study provides some comparisons of not only the differences between ideal behavior and actual behavior, but also a comparison of elementary and secondary school principals.

As shown in Figure 2.1, elementary school principals indicated that ideally they should spend 35 percent of their time in the areas of instructional improvement and only 12 percent in student services. However, they

Figure 2.1
Percentage of Time Elementary and Secondary School
Principals Devote to the Major Dimensions of Their Jobs:
Ideal vs. Actual Time Expended

Job Dimensions	Percentage of Time Spent on Job Dimensions			
	Elementary Principals		Secondary Principals	
	Ideal	Actual	Ideal	Actual
Improvement of instruction	35	24	27	17
Community relations	14	16	15	14
Student services	12	21	24	40
Operations	9	13	10	14
Evaluation	30	26	24	15

reported actually spending 24 percent and 21 percent, respectively. They spent less time than they thought they should on improving instruction and more time on maintaining the school (student services and operations). Similar discrepancies between actual and ideal time were found for secondary school principals in instructional improvement activities and student services.

Thus, several studies show that the answer to our first question is that principals do, indeed, regard instructional and program improvement as the most important aspects of their job. Nevertheless, they spend the greatest amount of their time on school management and operations, the dimensions they value least.

The second question of importance is how the average principal spends her time compared to the principal who is an instructional leader. Our studies have provided us with a profile of an average principal that we can compare to data gathered from principals who are considered to be instructional leaders. A considerable amount of work has been done in the past few years to more clearly define the role of the principal as instructional leader. The most reliable and valid of these efforts—those that have linked an operational definition of instructional leadership to incremental growth in student academic achievement—have identified the four areas of strategic interaction between principals and teachers that are explained in Chapter 1: resource provider, instructional resource, communicator, and visible presence.

Using this definition, in 1986 we selected a sample of school districts in the Pacific Northwest and asked the superintendents in those districts to nominate principals who they considered to be instructional leaders. We then asked a group of principals who were peers of these principals if they knew principals who they considered to be instructional leaders. Where there was concurrence between superintendent nominations and fellow principals' nominations, we contacted those principals to obtain permission to measure staff perceptions of their performance as instructional leaders. A total of 28 principals were included for analysis. Twenty-five of the 28 principals agreed to allow us to administer a questionnaire developed as part of an effective schools project, which has a key factor that measures teachers' perceptions of their principal as an instructional leader. The instrument was administered during a regularly scheduled staff meeting in the spring of 1986.

For a principal to be considered a "strong" instructional leader by the staff, the principal had to score at least one standard deviation above an average principal on the measure of instructional leadership. Of the principals nominated, 21 qualified (based on staff perceptions) as strong instructional leaders. That is, using the mean score and standard deviation derived from a sample of approximately 250 principals over a two-year period of time, they had a mean score of 82 or greater on a scale from 19 to 95. The sample of principals who qualified for the study consisted of 5 high school, 5 middle school, and 11 elementary school principals. These principals administered schools ranging in size from a 2,600-student high school to a 125-student elementary school. Eleven principals were female and 10 were male. Their administrative experience ranged from 3 years to over 16. Each of these principals agreed to keep a time log of daily activities using the methodology developed by Andrews and Hallett. A synthesis of conclusions from various studies suggests that principals believe the most important part of their job is educational program improvement, followed by school-community relations, student-related services and activities, building management and operations, and district relations. Using these rankings, a comparison of how the average principal spends her or his day, constructed from data gathered from the 1,006 principals in the Andrews and Hallett study, and how these 21 strong instructional leader principals spent time on a day-to-day basis are presented in Figure 2.2.

Figure 2.2 shows that the principals who were perceived as strong instructional leaders spent time quite differently from the average principal. Average principals consider educational program improvement as the part of the job that should receive the greatest amount of their time and energy; however, they spend more time on management (39 percent) and student services (28 percent) than they do on educational improvement (27 percent)

Figure 2.2
Percentage of Time Average Principals and Strong
Instructional Leaders Devote to the Major Dimensions
of Their Jobs

Job Dimensions	Percentage of Time Spent on Job Dimensions	
	Average Principals	Strong Instructional Leaders
Educational program improvement	27	41
School-community relations	6	7
Student-related services and activities	28	18
Building management, operations, and district relations	39	34
Average hours per day	10 +	10.75 +

activities. Average principals do not implement their values on a day-to-day basis as they allocate time among the various tasks that must be performed. This fact has lead observers of principals' management practices to conclude that many principals are "building managers" rather than "instructional leaders," and they should spend less time on building management and more time on improving instruction.

However, the data in Figure 2.2 suggest that principals who are strong instructional leaders do not divert time away from building management functions in favor of instructional leadership functions. In fact, they spend almost exactly the same amount of time on management functions, 3.7 hours per day (34% × 10.75 hrs.), as does the average principal who spends 3.9 hours per day (39% × 10.1 hrs.). Strong instructional leaders spend considerably less time on student-related activities, 1.9 hours per day (18% × 10.75 hrs.), compared to the average principal who spends 2.8 hours per day (28% × 10.1 hrs.), or nearly an hour less. The average principal spends only about 2.7 hours a day on curriculum and instruction issues, staff selection and evaluation, and supervision of staff. Strong instructional leaders spend 4.4 hours per day (41% × 10.75 hrs.) in this same category. These data suggest that principals who are strong instructional leaders implement discretionary time in such a way that they codify, on a day-to-day basis, the ideals or values of the average principal. They spend the greatest amount of their time on educational program improvement activities. These data also suggest that it is a false dichotomy to draw the distinction between being a strong building manager and a strong instructional leader. These 21 principals are both strong building managers and strong instructional leaders.

Our attempts to understand what the average principal does every day and what principals who are considered to be instructional leaders do every day suggest that principals who are instructional leaders are able to organize their day so they focus their time and attention on instructional matters rather than the routine matters of running the school. Thus, the issue for the average principal is not misplaced values but a poor allocation of discretionary time, or simply poor behavioral patterns.

We are frequently asked if secondary and elementary school principals differ in what they see as important in their jobs and how they spend their time. In our earlier work (Andrews and Hallett 1983a, 1983b), we found no differences in what principals considered of greatest or least value in their activities, although we did find differences in how they spent their time. For example, middle/junior high school principals spent more time in student-related activities than did senior high or elementary school principals. In addition, high school principals tended to spend more time in the management functions than did their elementary school counterparts. The differences in time allocations, however, were mostly in the least important aspects of the job, not the most important aspect—educational program improvement. We also found that female principals spent more time in educational program improvement activities than did male principals.

Since this question of differences between secondary and elementary principals has been of such great interest, Wing has just completed a study that was adapted from our work on the 21 strong instructional leaders and examined the allocation of time of these 21 principals based on type of school (high, middle/junior, and elementary). Her findings, contrasted with those of Andrews and Hallett's concerning the average elementary, middle/junior high, and high school principal, are presented in Figure 2.3.

The Wing findings are consistent with our study of all principals in that, regardless of whether the principals were from elementary, middle/junior high, or high schools, strong instructional leaders spent more time in educational program improvement activities than did the average principals in the Andrews and Hallett study. However, there are some differences among the three groups of principals in the Wing study.

All of the strong instructional leader principals spent less time with student-related activities than did the average principal, but the differences were greater for elementary and middle/junior high principals and the average principal than they were for the high school principals. In addition, the elementary and middle/junior high school principals spent more time on educational program improvement than did the high school principals. Further, the high school principals in the strong instructional leader group still spent more time on management and operations functions than they did on educational program improvement. These data suggest that there are some fundamental differences between high schools and elementary and middle/junior highs that force high school principals to spend less discretionary time on educational program improvement activities.

The data also suggest that principals who are perceived as strong instructional leaders spend their time differently from the average principal. And although there are differences in the distribution of time among the various aspects of the job, strong instructional leaders spend more time on instructional improvement activities than do average principals and less time handling student problems. There is little difference, however, in the amount of time strong instructional leaders spend on building management functions as compared to average principals. The fact that there are differences in the amount of time spent by strong instructional leaders on program and instructional improvement activities compared to the average principal prompts the question: Is it only a matter of time, or are there qualitative differences in the way average principals and strong instructional leaders spend their time?

Figure 2.3
Comparison of Percentage of Time Spent by Strong Instructional Leaders at the Elementary, Middle/Junior High, and High School Levels with the Average Principal for the Same Type of School

Job Dimensions of the School Principal Ranked by Importance	Principals by Type of School			
	All Schools*	Elem. Schools**	Middle Schools*	High Schools**
A. Educational Program Improvement				
Average Principal	27	28	23	25
Strong Leader	41	49	44	33
B. School-Community Relations				
Average Principal	6	7	5	8
Strong Leader	7	8	7	8
C. Student-Related Services and Activities				
Average Principal	28	26	35	26
Strong Leader	18	20	22	21
D. Building Management, Operations, and District Relations				
Average Principal	39	39	37	41
Strong Leader	34	23	27	38
Total Time Spent (hours in an average day)				
Average Principal	10.1	9.5	10.0	10.6
Strong Leader	10.75	10.7	10.8	10.8

*Andrews and Hallett study: n = 1,006; 58% were elementary, 18% middle/junior high, 16% senior high, and 8% mixed level (e.g., K–12, K–8, 7–12).

**Wing study: n = 21; 11 elementary, 5 middle/junior high, and 5 senior high schools.

More Than a Matter of Time

To discover whether the distribution of time between strong instructional leaders and average principals was the only difference between the two groups, we asked 1,100 teachers in strong, average, and weak instructional leader schools which of these activities and behaviors they regard as the most important for a principal to be considered a strong instructional leader and to describe the activities and behavior their principals practice daily that cause them to believe their principal is a strong instructional leader.

In responding to the phrase, "My principal is a strong instructional leader," teachers tend to agree with each of 18 specific, supporting statements. In addition, when teachers perceive their principals to be above average on these items, incremental growth in student academic achievement also tends to be high. When teachers perceive their principals to be below average on these same items, incremental growth in student academic achievement tends to be low (Andrews and Soder 1987a, 1987b). These 18 statements are the core descriptors for the four areas of strategic interaction that define the principal as a strong instructional leader—resource provider, instructional resource, communicator, and visible presence.

In the remainder of this chapter, we present the areas of strategic interaction, their key descriptors, and the teachers' perceptions about strong, average, and weak leaders.

The Principal as Resource Provider

Figure 2.4 indicates the teachers' ratings of their principals using four descriptors of the principal as a resource provider.

The data in Figure 2.4 suggest that not all teachers in schools administered by strong instructional leaders see principals as fulfilling the re-

Figure 2.4
How Teachers Rate Their Principal as Resource Provider

| | Percentage of Positive Ratings | | |
| | Strong Leader ($n = 800$) | Average Leader ($n = 2,146$) | Weak Leader ($n = 300$) |
Job Dimensions			
1. My principal promotes staff development activities for teachers.	95	68	41
2. My principal is knowledgeable about instructional resources.	90	54	33
3. My principal mobilizes resources and district support to help achieve academic achievement goals.	90	52	33
4. My principal is considered an important instructional resource person in this school.	79	35	8

32

source-provider role. However, on each of the subdimensions, the overwhelming majority of teachers have positive perceptions of the strong instructional leader. The percentage of teachers who perceive their principal positively decreases across the three groups. The greatest difference is whether the teachers see the principal as an "important instructional resource." Two of the subdimensions of resource provider are considered more important than other subdimensions: "Mobilizes resources and district support to help achieve academic goals," and "Promotes staff development activities for teachers."

On a day-to-day operations level, school principals who are seen as strong resource providers do not regard the school budget as an expenditure plan that constrains them from acting but as an allocation to be expanded. Their staff sees them as viewing the entire school community and district as possessing potential resources for use in the school, and that it is the principal's job to get these resources, which he does. They are perceived as never saying no to staff members' ideas. They know people, research, and new things about education. They use staff members as staff developers and peer coaches for other staff members. In response to teachers who want to improve their skills in a specific area, they frequently say, "I will get you out of your class to do this, even if it means I take your class!" and, "Once you get this special training, you can train other staff members in our school."

The Principal as Instructional Resource

Figure 2.5 shows teachers' perceptions of their principals in four subdimensions.

Just as not all teachers in schools administered by strong instructional leaders see them as fulfilling the resource provider role, not all teachers see them as an instructional resource. However, the overwhelming majority of teachers perceive the strong instructional leader principal positively in this area. Of note is the lack of variation among the three groups on the encouragement of the use of different instructional strategies. However, the similarity in response stops there. Our analysis of teachers' comments suggests a clear difference between *how* strong instructional leaders and weak principals encourage teachers to use different strategies.

The principal's ability to help teachers expand their use of instructional strategies is key to improving the school. The primary, and maybe the only, place that the principal has the opportunity to improve instruction is during a conference with a teacher after a clinical observation of a teaching episode. Teachers interpret the behavior of principals as positive in that they will provide teachers with a shopping list of different strategies and

Figure 2.5
How Teachers Rate Their Principal as Instructional Resource

	Percentage of Positive Ratings		
Job Dimensions	Strong Leader ($n = 800$)	Average Leader ($n = 2,146$)	Weak Leader ($n = 300$)
1. My principal encourages the use of different instructional strategies.	89	78	75
2. My principal is sought out by teachers who have instructional concerns or problems.	72	47	25
3. My principal's evaluation of my performance helps improve my teaching.	78	46	17
4. My principal helps faculty interpret test results.	54	35	9

encourage them to try them. Strong instructional leaders, however, encourage the use of different strategies and serve as cheerleaders, encouragers, facilitators, counselors, and coaches for expanding the teacher's repertoire of instructional strategies one step at a time. During the post-observation conference, the strong instructional leader principal asks, "What are some other ways that you might have taught this same concept?" She then helps the teacher identify a new teaching strategy that the teacher feels comfortable trying and says something on the order of, "Why don't you try it? It's okay if it doesn't work," or "Let me know when you are going to use the strategy and I'll come and watch you do it. We'll sit down right afterward and talk about how it went. If it doesn't work, we'll work on trying something else."

Principal as Communicator

The third strategic area of interaction is for the principal to be seen as a good communicator at three different levels—one-on-one, as a small-group facilitator, and to create a sense of vision for the school. Here there are six important areas of interaction, as presented in Figure 2.6.

The areas that define the importance of communication provide a clear picture of the differences among average, weak, and strong instructional leaders. In all categories except "Provides frequent feedback regarding classroom performance," 80 percent or more of the teachers perceived the strong leaders in a positive light. The percentages were, in the

Figure 2.6
How Teachers Rate Their Principal as Communicator

| | Percentage of Positive Ratings | | |
Job Dimensions	Strong Leader ($n = 800$)	Average Leader ($n = 2,146$)	Weak Leader ($n = 300$)
1. Improved instructional practice results from interactions with my principal.	80	49	25
2. My principal leads formal discussions concerning instruction and student achievement.	85	41	17
3. My principal uses clearly communicated criteria for judging staff performance.	90	63	17
4. My principal provides a clear vision of what our school is all about.	90	49	17
5. My principal communicates clearly to the staff regarding instructional matters.	92	50	17
6. My principal provides frequent feedback to teachers regarding classroom performance.	68	29	18

main, below 50 percent for the average principal, and below 20 percent for the weak leader principal group for the same items. Teachers typically said that strong instructional leaders clearly communicate the message "Try new things with students—it's okay if they don't work. If something does not work, try something else." They also communicate a sense of professionalism to their staff members by clinically supervising them according to their performance as teachers. They tend to characterize their teachers as superstars; good, strong, average teachers; and low-performing, marginally competent, or incompetent teachers. They do not violate the integrity of the clinical supervision model with any group, but they vary the clinical model based on the performance level of the teacher. This is described more fully in Chapter 5.

Strong instructional leaders are able to spend less time on student matters because they work to improve the skills of all teachers, particularly low-performing teachers. Each is described by their teachers as tough, fair, and a "tyrant" for kids. They prefer to counsel teachers rather than evaluate teachers out of teaching. However, they articulate the view that they will use whichever method works. Teachers perceive that their principals expect a high level of performance from their teaching staff, and they model high performance standards in their own behavior.

"Providing a clear vision of what the school is all about" is more important to teachers than most of the other activities that describe instructional leaders. Teachers report that strong instructional leader principals start the school year with statements like, "I have spent my summer thinking about our school, reviewing our curriculum and instructional methods, reviewing new ideas about education, reviewing the performance of our students." Then they either say, "Here is where I think we should go this year, and we are going to spend the afternoon gaining consensus about what we are going to do, and each of us must commit ourselves to doing it," or they say, "Here is where I have decided we are going this year. Anyone who does not want to go there with us, we'll find someplace else for you to go!" The teachers in these schools believe their principals all yell "CHARGE!" but clearly they each yell Charge! in their own way, based on personal style and the way they work with the teachers in their school.

The Principal as Visible Presence

The fourth strategic area of interaction concerns the principal's visible presence in the school. Strong instructional leader principals are seen as "visionaries who are out and around." Their presence is created by day-to-day behavior that is consistent with their values. For example, if they expect a clean, well-kept building, they do not pass paper on the floor in the hall without picking it up. They can espouse a philosophy about education and their school while at the same time going about the more mundane routine of running the school. They have a keen understanding of how that philosophy must be "played out" daily in the school.

The four important descriptors of interaction in the visible presence area are presented in Figure 2.7.

Just as in the other three areas of interaction, the data in Figure 2.7 suggest that not all teachers see strong instructional leaders in positive terms. However, for each descriptor, the overwhelming majority of teachers—and in all cases except one, over 90 percent of the teachers—perceive positively the strong instructional leader principal. However, the differences between the percentage of teachers who see the average principal and the weak principal compared to the strong leader principal are not as great for visible measure as are the differences in the other areas of strategic interaction—particularly when seen as communicator. The greatest difference among the three groups of principals is the degree to which they

Figure 2.7
How Teachers Rate Their Principal as Visible Presence

	Percentage of Positive Ratings		
Job Dimensions	Strong Leader ($n = 800$)	Average Leader ($n = 2,146$)	Weak Leader ($n = 300$)
1. My principal makes frequent classroom observations.	72	31	17
2. My principal is accessible to discuss matters dealing with instruction.	94	68	66
3. My principal is a "visible presence" in the building to both staff and students.	93	75	46
4. My principal is an active participant in staff development activities.	97	64	50

make "frequent classroom observations." The extent to which the principal creates a visible presence in the school to both the staff and students is the most important factor for the principal to be seen as a strong instructional leader by teachers.

On a day-to-day operations level, there are two levels on which principals present a strong, visible presence. First, they are seen out and around in classrooms, in the lunchroom, in hallways during passing time, with the buses before and after school, and in assemblies. They make positive announcements over the public address system in the morning before instruction begins and praise the staff and students for good work. At the elementary school level, these principals do not feel their day is successful *unless they are in every classroom every day*. At the middle/junior high and senior high school levels, the principals do not consider their week to have been successful *unless they are in every classroom during the week*.

When they are out and around in classrooms, "passing through," they respond to what they observe only with praise. Some use small note cards, others catch the teacher in the lunchroom or hallway and provide positive feedback, others drop a note in the teacher's mailbox. When the principal picks up something negative in a classroom, she schedules an extended observation in that teacher's classroom later in the day or the next day. The reason for the extended observation is to deal with the negative behavior identified in the "pass through." Teachers want these principals in their classrooms because they get only praise as a result of the principal's "passing through" activities.

More important, their presence is felt, whether they are in the building or not, by a deeply ingrained philosophy of education that permeates the school. Staff, students, and parents know what these principals stand for in education. They live and breathe their philosophy about education. They have a keen sense of how to translate educational philosophy into words and deeds so that it is visible for all to see.

Getting a Handle on the Principal's Time

Observations of the average principal and the strong instructional leader suggest that they both value the same things about their jobs, but the strong instructional leader is not as distracted by the routine parts of the job as the average principal. The strong instructional leader focuses on the curriculum and instructional matters. Thus, the amount of time that the principal spends on the various dimensions of the job are important. In the Appendix are time analysis record sheets and a Zero-Based Job Description Questionnaire looking at the time distribution of the average principal and the strong instructional leader principal. These documents can help individuals analyze their values, how they spend their time, and identify areas that need restructuring to ensure greater focus on instructional improvement.

3

Expectations of an Instructional Leader

For principals to improve their skills as instructional leaders, superintendents and other district-level administrators must practice new supervisory behaviors, such as role modeling, and enlightened strategies that encourage professional growth and provide needed organizational support. Our work with such a supervisory model in two school districts (one with 16,000 students and another with 3,000 students) over nine years has convinced us that strong, supportive supervision of school principals can be a significant factor in promoting school reform and improvement practices.

Referent power, motivation, and high self-esteem strongly influence a principal's desire to change behavior and practice new skills that will reinforce that change over time (Lovell and Wiles 1983, Herzberg, Mausner, and Snyderman 1959, Sergiovanni 1975). Referent power is the supervisor's influence as a "reference" or resource. Through modeling, demonstration, and collegial practice, the supervisor works with the principal over a long period of time to foster growth in skills and encourage needed practice with feedback. In addition, motivation and high self-esteem are linked with successful performance. The highest motivators of job performance are achievement, recognition, the work itself, and responsibility (Herzberg, Mausner, and Snyderman 1959)—all of which can be accommodated through a clinical supervision model that involves the principal and the supervisor in a collegial, collaborative relationship.

Building a successful supervisory relationship with the principal requires the supervisor to develop a level of trust that will accommodate the principal's human needs associated with learning complex skills. As noted by Knowles (1978) and Bents and Howey (1981), adults learn best when their staff-development activities recognize their needs and interests, are organized around life situations, are experience-based, engage them in a process of mutual inquiry, and provide for differences in learning style and rate. Petrie and Burton (1980) posit that leaders progress through developmental levels of learning as they gain experience and expertise. These levels range along a continuum of supervisory behaviors, from establishing routines and rules to stimulating others' development. Further, the educator's level of commitment to the profession, along with her ability to think conceptually, affects the supervisor's ability to stimulate needed changes in behavior (Glickman 1981, Glatthorn 1984).

The research of Joyce and Showers (1983) and Wood and Thompson (AASA 1980) suggests that principals, like teachers, should be involved in the design, delivery, and evaluation of their professional development. Training must provide theoretical and practical components, with follow-up coaching over time to help principals understand the reasons for behavioral changes and to practice new skills in the real-world setting of their schools. Principals must be able to practice the new behaviors, engage in dialogue that helps them analyze and evaluate their own performance, and gain control of the new behaviors until they can use them as needed.

Because the principal's role is changing from that of building manager or administrator to instructional leader, the principal requires ongoing, substantive staff development and support to refine, extend, and evaluate his supervisory skills. A deliberate sequence of clinical supervision can provide the analysis and evaluation that will help improve performance.

Such a sequence, based on clear performance expectations, provides guidance, practice, and support for the principal's development of requisite skills. And it enables the principal to evaluate her own clinical supervision of the teaching staff through a series of observations and interactive feedback sessions. Clinical supervision ensures quality control while maximizing opportunities for the principal to delegate authority and leadership. It is also an effective tool for the supervisor when the principal's performance is unsatisfactory.

Five basic assumptions are key to the successful use of our clinical supervision model for the principal's supervisor. All supervisory activities build on these assumptions.

1. The goal of clinical supervision is the improvement of instruction. As the principal uses clinical supervision to work collegially with the teaching staff, her skills in instruction should be enhanced.

2. Process and product are valued in the clinical supervision model for principals. Attention must be given to processes, communication, and engagement, as well as to products, outcomes, and results obtained, as measured by changes in teacher behaviors and attitudes.

3. The principal must play a major role in her own evaluation. Professionals who are involved in the design, delivery, and assessment of their professional development are more likely to change their behavior.

4. Specified criteria, along with individual performance goals, are the basis for evaluating the principal's performance. Clear expectations and standards are as essential for the improvement of the principal's performance as they are for student learning.

5. *Supervision* is the overarching set of behaviors that characterize the supervisor-principal relationship; *evaluation* is the highest level of cognition, essential to professional development. Evaluation is a cognitive process that compares performance to a standard and identifies strengths and weaknesses to give direction for future efforts. Both formative and summative evaluative processes are necessary components of performance evaluation. The processes associated with supervision and evaluation are intertwined, interrelated, and inseparable.

Defining Expectations of an Instructional Leader

We hold high expectations for principals' performance as instructional leaders. However, merely holding such expectations is not sufficient; they must be made explicitly clear to the principal in word and deed. This benefits the principal and the supervisor alike, for it focuses effort and attention on priority activities. Our expectations for the principal's performance follow the four major categories of activities presented in Chapter 1 in the definition of an instructional leader: resource provider, instructional resource, communicator, and visible presence.

Resource Provider

Human resources are key to effective schools; therefore, the principal is expected to treat the staff with the highest respect and care. Teachers are assigned with regard for their teaching expertise. Care is given to balancing teaching teams, grade levels, or departments to provide a variety of styles and approaches. The school schedule reflects the artistic development of the staff and provides a flexible framework that permits routine, daily interaction among professionals. District staff members are incorporated into the school's team of professionals, providing support and special expertise at the principal's request.

The principal provides instructional materials adequate for the staff to deliver the curriculum, including textbooks, supplies, and equipment. The budget reflects the priorities of the school, and the staff contributes to its development. The principal has a clear grasp of district and building finances so that this information can be shared with the teachers as they help design each year's instructional budget. Information of all sorts constantly is shared with staff—insights from professional journals, district items of interest, parents' concerns. Staff, parent, and student advisory groups contribute to the decisions that govern that school. People feel valued for their opinions and express pride and ownership in the school. Finally, the principal is always alert for external resources to link with the school's resources, and staff development options are made available.

How, then, does the principal's supervisor assess the degree to which expectations are being fulfilled and the areas in which inservice training or remediation measures are needed? One way is to collect and observe some specific outcomes, behaviors, and "artifacts." For example, the following indicators can be used to evaluate the principal's performance as resource provider.

1. Teaching assignments match the expertise of the staff.

2. The master schedule gives team teachers common planning periods.

3. School- and district-level staff members work together to assess student needs or to develop curriculums.

4. A sufficient supply of materials is maintained and stored in organized and accessible areas.

5. Records of meetings show how staff members have been involved in budget decisions.

6. Staff meetings are organized as instructional episodes, with the principal serving as a teacher or facilitator, encouraging participation through use of small- and large-group processes.

7. Practitioners' workshops, retreats, and sharing of new ideas show the principal's leadership in seeking additional resources and opportunities.

Instructional Resource

The principal should wholeheartedly practice clinical supervision, "supervision up close" (Goldhammer 1969). The purpose of frequent classroom observations and dialogues with teachers is the improvement of instruction. An ongoing conversation about students' learning and teachers' teaching methods focuses on the mission of the school. Teachers may be observed seeking out the principal for ideas or to be a sounding board for their ideas about teaching. A variety of observational methods are employed throughout the school, and all staff members are involved in some way with colleagues in peer observations and "coaching" or idea sharing. As with Little's (1982) "norms of collegiality," the culture of the school reflects a bias for change and an adaptation of teaching styles and strategies to meet the needs of the students. Staff evaluation is perceived as a natural complement to the clinical supervision processes, and the teachers and principal take part in evaluating their own and their colleagues' teaching performance (Alfonso and Goldsberry 1982).

Central to the supervision and evaluation model used here is Bolton's (1973, 1980) conceptualization of a cyclical model with three well-defined phases: planning for evaluation, collecting information, and using information (Figure 3.1, p. 44). At the heart of this model is the idea that evaluation is an ongoing process.

During Phase I, goals are established by the school as a whole and by each teacher. At the beginning of the year, each teacher establishes personal performance goals related to school, district, and individual priorities. Strategies and action plans are identified and calendared. As part of the evaluation design, the principal and teacher identify means for collecting data and assessing progress and achievement. During the course of the year, the principal completes a series of clinical supervision cycles that include pre-observation discussions, classroom observations, and post-observation feedback conferences. These activities are included in Bolton's Phase II, data collection. The cycles represent one method of gathering data about the teacher's performance that year.

About halfway through the year, the principal and teacher discuss progress on the annual goals and, if necessary, adjust or revise them. The principal has the opportunity to suggest alternative resources or to provide support to the teacher who may have had difficulty with one or more of the goals. At the end of the school year, Phase III includes a final conference to discuss the data that have been collected by both parties. Collaboratively, the principal and teacher decide which goals have been achieved and how the teacher's performance measures up to the standard criteria. They establish some tentative goals for the upcoming year.

Not every teacher benefits from a standard supervisory approach (Glickman 1981), and principals should vary their approach according to the needs and style of each teacher. For most, the collaborative approach will prove most effective. For a few individuals, a direct approach with specific "assignments" is more beneficial. The direct approach is recom-

Figure 3.1
Bolton's Three-Phase, Cyclical Process for Evaluating Personnel
(Bolton 1973)

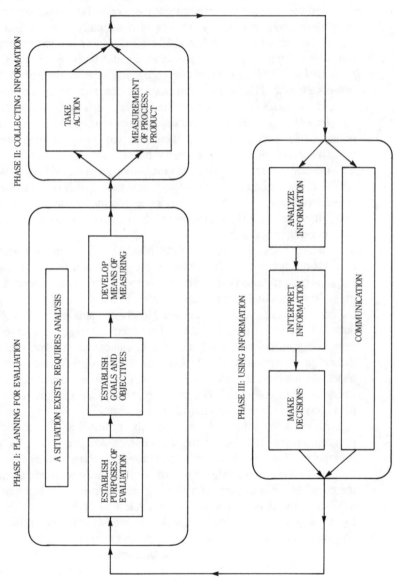

PHASE I: PLANNING FOR EVALUATION

A SITUATION EXISTS, REQUIRES ANALYSIS

ESTABLISH PURPOSES OF EVALUATION

ESTABLISH GOALS AND OBJECTIVES

DEVELOP MEANS OF MEASURING

PHASE II: COLLECTING INFORMATION

TAKE ACTION

MEASUREMENT OF PROCESS, PRODUCT

PHASE III: USING INFORMATION

MAKE DECISIONS

INTERPRET INFORMATION

ANALYZE INFORMATION

COMMUNICATION

mended for new teachers or for those who require remediation. For other individuals, a nondirective approach may provide the most supportive supervision. These teachers, called "professionals" by Glickman (1981) and "omnivores" by Joyce, Hersh, and McKibbin (1983), respond to a supportive, hands-off approach that puts them in a leadership role in the design of their own evaluation plan.

These and other examples of evidence can be used to evaluate the principal as an instructional resource:

1. Teachers discuss instructional issues in the staff room and with the principal.

2. The principal maintains a checklist for classroom observations, noting dates and frequencies. The goal is to complete one clinical supervision cycle per day.

3. Accurate, timely write-ups of post-observation conferences are given to the teacher, and a copy is kept for the principal's reference.

4. Teachers are involved in the examination and analysis of observed data.

5. Teachers collaborate with the principal in the design, data collection, and analysis and evaluation phases of their own annual performance evaluation.

6. Teachers observe in each others' classrooms and give helpful feedback to each other. The principal supports this activity by providing release time through budgeting for substitutes or by taking a teacher's class from time to time. A record may be kept of such activities, and budget reports show the way resources have been directed toward this activity.

7. Each teacher's evaluation design, including annual goals, is available for review.

8. The annual written evaluation for each teacher reflects highlights of this unique year, goal accomplishment, performance evaluated against established criteria, and tentative goals for the year to come.

9. The principal is specific and assertive in following contractual and legal requirements for teacher probation and performance remediation. Staff members whose performance is judged to be deficient receive intensive support, and the process results in either improved performance or termination of employment.

Communicator

Communicating effectively in an organization requires skills beyond the interpersonal level. As instructional leader, the principal must be able to develop a sound and trusting relationship with the staff by behaving consistently, objectively, and fairly over time. Rules for communicating must be made explicit regarding the content and the processes that are acceptable within the culture of that school. What topics, for example, may be discussed openly by the entire staff? By parent-staff advisory groups? By students and staff? By supervisor-teacher dyads? What structures and processes will be used by what groups to make which decisions about governance of the school? To what degree will autonomy be given to the staff in the decision-making process? Which decisions will be made by the principal after asking for staff input and advice? How do building decisions fit into the scheme of the school district's processes? All of these questions should be answered through the principal's leadership and communication with the staff (Smith 1989).

Processes are all-important. The principal models commitment to those processes in establishing school goals together with the staff, parents, and students. Resources are committed to the goals, and evaluation systems are established. Frequent reference is made to the goals, and classroom observations, inservice topics, and faculty meetings focus on those priorities.

A clear vision for the school is articulated by the principal to the point of redundancy. Through slogans, themes, logos, and reminders, the principal makes it known that everyone in this school is headed in the same general direction. Individual teachers may choose different means of achieving this, emphasizing different strengths and interests, but the overarching direction supersedes individual whim.

Frequent feedback is given to teachers after classroom visits, to custodians and secretaries after performance observations or special contributions, to students for achievements of all kinds, and to parents for their support and efforts. Further, the principal employs a consistent "feedback loop" to tell those involved in the decision-making processes how their input or involvement affected the final outcome or decision. Regular bulletins and newsletters are published for the staff, parents, and students.

Each year, the principal reviews the expectations for staff performance and the system to be employed for clinical supervision and evaluation. Roles of peer observers and coaches are clarified. Staff members are involved in establishing priorities for inservice training and staff development activities. Faculty meetings are well-organized "instructional episodes." The principal has clear objectives, involves participants to promote learning of the objectives, adjusts the time or process to meet needs that arise during the meeting, and has methods for closing the meeting to be sure everyone understands what was discussed. Careful planning for all meetings ensures they are worthwhile and do not waste time on items that can be handled elsewhere.

Data that may be used to assess the principal's performance as communicator include:

1. Written procedures for making school decisions delineate clearly what content will be discussed by what groups to what outcome.

2. Staff meetings are well organized and reflect careful planning with regard to objectives, activities, participation, and closure.

3. School goals are publicized in a variety of ways. They are referenced by the principal in budget allocations, newsletters, and reports to the supervisor. Teachers and parents can verbalize the school's goals.

4. The school's vision is publicized overtly through themes, logos, or statements.

5. Written messages are given to the staff, parents, and students by the principal as recognition for their accomplishments.

6. Individual staff members can describe the evaluation system and the principal's expectations for their performances.

Visible Presence

The principal who is visible in the school truly seems to be everywhere: in hallways, staff rooms, classrooms, the boiler room, the cafeteria; at the bus loading area at strategic times; at school plays, sporting events, concerts, and other special programs. Always there at assemblies, the principal helps to reinforce standards of behavior and supports faculty and student participation.

Visible principals do many things at once. On the way down the hall to visit a classroom, she talks with several students, a teacher, and a custodian. A handy note pad may be used en route to jot down things to do or remember.

The principal's secretary is polite but firm when parents or others appear in the office and ask to see the principal. The response might be, "Ms. Johnson is observing in a classroom for the next hour. May I schedule an appointment for you when she returns?" Never does the secretary remark, "Oh, she isn't at her desk now."

The day begins early for the principal, who makes a quick walkthrough to greet custodians and the kitchen staff. Special events or jobs of the day can be described to staff members ahead of time.

Drop-in classroom visits are frequent, and the principal enjoys talking with students about their work, assisting some, or participating in a class activity. Because such visits are a familiar occurrence, the teacher and students seldom vary their routine to acknowledge the principal's presence. Clearly, the principal belongs in this setting.

Frequently the principal participates in staff development or inservice courses. In fact, the principal attempts to learn new curriculum content or a teaching skill by practicing in staff meetings or classrooms and talking about those experiences with staff. During classroom observations, the principal may ask to see the teacher use one of the skills from a workshop or to teach some aspect of content being emphasized.

A number of examples illustrate ways in which the supervisor can evaluate the principal's skills at being a visible presence:

1. Drop-in visits to the school find the principal "out walking around the campus" or visiting classrooms.

2. Attending student assemblies on occasion, the supervisor notes how the principal interacts with students and the staff.

3. Shadowing the principal for a day reveals the methods by which several things are accomplished at once.

4. The secretary often tells the supervisor that the principal is "out in the classrooms" or "in the cafeteria."

5. When dropping in classrooms with the principal, the supervisor notes that students and the staff go about their business as usual.

6. The principal makes a staff development activity one performance goal for the year. He demonstrates a new skill for the supervisor.

In this chapter we've seen the kinds of behaviors that can be expected of principals who are instructional leaders. In the next chapter, we take a closer look at seven real principals who are living up to those expectations in their daily routines.

4

Instructional Leaders
in Action

Many principals are already instructional leaders, and we turn now to seven who are providing instructional leadership for their schools at the elementary, middle, and senior high levels. These seven were identified during the design of a new program[1] at the University of Washington for preparing school principals as instructional leaders. The anecdotes in this chapter are based on information from teams of educators who observed and gathered data in the principals' schools.[2]

As you study these principals, note the clear differences in their styles. For example, at the high school level we have Al, who is seen as quiet and reflective; nothing seems to ruffle his feathers. Al is not a newcomer to the school district where he is principal but has a long family connection to the community he serves. Another principal, Jan, is seen as

---

[1]Details about the design of this program, which was funded by a grant from the Danforth Foundation, are set forth in "The Danforth Program for the Preparation of School Leaders," available from the University of Washington, College of Education, Seattle, WA 98195.

[2]The three-member teams included professors, graduate students, and public school administrators who were trained in portraiture methodology, developed by Sara Lawrence Lightfoot and explained in *Good High School Portraits of Character and Culture* (New York: Basic Books, 1985). The seven principals selected for description here were among the teams' portraitures of 23 schools.

a no-nonsense, data-driven leader. Both impressed us as examples of high school principals who have found their own way to overcome the barriers that many experience when attempting to be instructional leaders.

A Seed-Planting Viking

The home of the Vikings is the largest of three district high schools, serving 1,250 students in grades 10-12. Set in a predominantly white, middle-class community, the school population has only a dozen minority students. The district is growing, and the old and new are juxtaposed, illustrating what the area was and what it is becoming. Close by are new homes, apartment complexes, and condominiums; a dairy sign advertising fresh milk is evidence of a fading pastoral countryside. New multi-unit dwellings lie across the street from small, single-family homes constructed in the 1950s and '60s.

The high school campus, built in 1964, is located on a hill in the midst of a residential area, creating a quiet neighborhood atmosphere. The unjoined one-story buildings surround a courtyard with a center area like a Roman forum. Students congregate there at lunch, enjoying the sunshine or the company of friends. The separate buildings house each of the school's nine departments and a gym, cafeteria, library, and spacious counseling department.

The school principal, Al, in dress and demeanor, presents a solid, calm, neat appearance. The day of our interview, a Kiwanis pin adorned the lapel of his trim, navy blue blazer. His unruffled exterior is perhaps a reflection of an inner peace. "Nothing surprises him. He's very calm, easygoing. He has a wide comfort zone," say teachers. "Al's perspective on the job is: To show up for work and take what comes, you have to be flexible, you don't plan every minute." An outwardly kind and gentle person, Al frequently describes himself as quiet or shy. Yet both are attributes he has worked to overcome as an administrator. "I've had to learn how to perform, and I don't know which it is I prefer anymore." Teachers, parents, and students remark on his sense of humor. "Al jokes without losing respect. He maintains a balance but is a good sport." They reflect good-naturedly on a popular assembly where Al "does skits and will even get a pie in the face." Al is recognized as an integral part of the faculty.

Al is both a part and a product of his school district. The athletic field is named after his maternal grandfather, a local coach and teacher with high community standing. Al proudly describes the influence and example of his father and grandfather and of his grandmother, who was a teacher for 30 years. Al has carried on the tradition and is involved with a variety of community programs. He uses his connections to help kids by raising money for scholarships. As we approach the high school—a reconverted elementary school—Al points to the classroom where he attended 1st grade. His strong sense of school and community are interwoven into the fabric of his being. He "gets involved, puts personal time and effort in; it's not just a job, he makes it part of his life."

He learned to imitate outgoing qualities by watching his father. "I never felt as outgoing; he was a people person and I always respected that, but by being around him I naturally picked up some of those same tendencies over time." A sensitive person, he sometimes shelters feelings and may appear to some as aloof. He relates that the adage "still waters run deep" accurately portrays him. His struggle with his intuitive-reflective self and his outgoing side has given him a deep understanding for others. "In working with kids and teachers, [I have found that] those most reserved or resistant have strong feelings and they're not comfortable in showing it," says Al. Perhaps a parent best summarizes the personal characteristics of this principal: "He is strong, forthright, and energetic, a principled principal. Not affable, but that goes along with his demeanor."

The belief that everyone can learn permeates Al's philosophy. "Everybody can learn, and adults can change. You can teach an old dog new tricks if you give him a reason." Al supports teacher learning through a "lottery." Each Monday, he and his assistants draw a name from an envelope. The teacher selected is released for a half day to "obtain a learning experience elsewhere." Teachers attend workshops, read, or perform any activity of their choosing that helps them grow professionally. Teachers interviewed were enthusiastic about the lottery. "If teachers learn new things, that provides a good model for students." Al's high trust and regard for teachers as professionals is evident: he does not insist on a report of the release-time activity. "We are trusted and treated as professionals," note appreciative teachers.

Al himself models continued learning. "He is well read, always looking for something new, reaching out to learn more from other people and books. He keeps us a growing community, always being challenged." He photocopies educational articles of interest and places them in the faculty room. He talks with the different department heads to provide support for trying new ideas. Parents also comment on his knowledge. "He's very informed; [he] impresses you as a person interested in education. He reads research and is good at getting a point across backed up by good information." Students commend him as open to new ideas. "That's neat, I think," the Associated Student Body (ASB) vice president responds. Consistent with his beliefs that everyone can learn, Al "models professionalism."

Perhaps his most strongly held belief is also his most controversial. Al believes that people get hurt by labels. His feelings found articulation after he read a book on tracking. "When I read the Oakes book, it made sense why I've been feeling like I have." He tried to eliminate the bottom track so all kids feel like they are included in the student body. Students' self-worth is a priority for Al, and he cites one experience that shaped his belief: "One of my best friends struggled in school and now is running a multimillion-dollar corporation. But our valedictorian ended up in prison. It doesn't matter what someone's potential is, it's what they're doing at the moment." Al feels that tracking and labels put too much pressure on kids for grades, and there is a "need to get back to considering values."

Al's beliefs about tracking have influenced educational ideas and programs at this school. He talks about a special education student who inadvertently registered for algebra and got an A in the course because "nobody told her she couldn't." Everybody should be able to try something, he insists. He believes in encouraging students and not letting kids think they're not good enough.

Al notes that his experience supports the research that student involvement in activities correlates with future success. The school band, numbering 180 students, is a testimony to his encouragement of student activities. Many agree with his "vision of a well-rounded school." He does not "lump everybody in one group; he sees kids' individual needs and provides for them." One student, recently returned from drug treatment, expressed appreciation for the school's diversity. "A lot of schools focus on academics. This one has a lot of stuff for kids, like After Care" (a followup treatment program). A parent notes, "We have both ends of ability; his perspective is to find a place for everybody."

Not unexpectedly, the most disagreement with Al's philosophy of labeling and tracking comes from the accelerated/honors-class advocates. Over time, Al has decreased the number of honors classes. The vice president of the student body, among the dissenters, asserts, "He does not agree with accelerated programs, and I disagree with that. He thinks it labels people. He wants the strong to help the weak. I feel students are helped in accelerated programs as they go at their pace." He relates the problems capable students usually have with heterogeneous grouping, such as boredom, and the problems low-ability students have, such as frustration. Teachers may agree with protecting the less capable, but others agree with the ASB vice president that accelerated students get frustrated, too. "We don't see eye to eye," relates one teacher. "I like things more tracked. I think students should be challenged." Yet even those who disagree believe that Al truly has the interest of students at heart. "He tries to do things that make good educational sense. Some issues may not be well received, but he focuses on students and why we're here. He's sincere about it."

Al is spontaneously described as accessible, a good listener, trustworthy, and not wishy-washy. "He is diplomatic in getting results without offense." Accessibility is important to the staff; he is available and always there. Commenting on his ability to listen, some commend the depth of his attention. "You know you can come to him and suggest an alternative and he will seriously listen, not just give lip service. He will support you when deserving, but he will correct if necessary. He's very fair." Students, too, appreciate approachability. "He takes time out of the day to say, 'How are you?' He doesn't put himself on a big level." Another student notes a personal experience. "I got my purse stolen. I was crying and he talked to me, always listening with his eyes and ears. He helped me through that." Another person noted,. "Listening is one of his greatest qualities. He doesn't give me the impression that he's not hearing, even if he disagrees." A key secretary spoke for the classified group. "He talks to us, not at us. We feel very confident in him. He doesn't participate in gossip, cronyism, or the 'good ol' boy' network."

Many recognize that a principal has the power to help or harm through the distribution of resources. "When we go to him, he really listens to our request and if he can do it, he does. He is supportive of the music program." The head of the building inservice committee lamented that allocated money was spent for the year. "But," he said, "I know if someone comes in and wants to go somewhere I can say, 'Go see Al,' and he will use his discretionary fund."

During his first year as principal, Al created an ad hoc group to deal with faculty complaints. The Faculty Administration Communication Team (F.A.C.T.) was "a really positive thing." Faculty members could channel complaints anonymously to group members, who discussed concerns with Al and made minutes of their meeting public. The team is described as an effective vehicle for defusing situations and solving problems when a change disturbs the existing culture. It is also an example of how the school culture influences the principal. "I've had to learn a lot of patience instead of jumping to conclusions," Al says. The F.A.C.T. was instrumental in changing some of Al's views, both the staff and the principal concur. "Al had some misperceptions when he came here, and in time he saw some of the weaknesses as strengths." The F.A.C.T. rarely meets anymore—a result, notes Al, of problems being solved.

Al is often required to make a judgment call on a situation, and the staff notes his ability to work with ambiguity. "With Al, nothing is black or white: it's gray. Others have gone by the book. Al works in the gray area. He's flexible, tolerant." He is also noted for his one-on-one relationships. "He does a lot of contact work in the faculty room. He gets a tremendous amount of work done there. Al is never the last person to know anything."

He is open to risks and sincerely believes in improvement. Each year he asks the faculty to complete an anonymous, open-ended report on the year and their concerns. He makes it known that he values their honest response to two questions: "How has my performance met your expectations? What area should I devote more time to improving?" Of himself he says, "I wonder all of the time how I'm doing. I agonize over everything but if I feel a direction in my gut, I'll go for it."

The principal and the two assistants work closely together, meeting frequently to share ideas or solve problems. The staff and parents view the threesome as a unit. "It's not just he [the principal], but the administrative team." Some note the difficulty of talking about one without including the others. Al meets with his two assistants every Monday morning to discuss the week ahead, write the bulletin, and organize for the week. They frequently touch base throughout the day to monitor the progress of a problem discussed earlier. Al's penchant for sharing includes not only information and decision making but the credit as well. In return, he has the loyalty and respect of his team.

"Working well as a team" rated highly in the faculty year-end evaluation of the principal. Parents speak in team language and describe the administration in general. "It is a very supportive administrative staff. They respect me as a person and will listen. They are accessible."

Al's ability to delegate is frequently mentioned by the team as a strength and source of professional growth. "He gives me the ability to do what I need to do and doesn't restrict me. He doesn't say no, but encourages you to take it to the max." Administrative responsibilities are divided among the three. Each evaluates a third of the teaching staff and assumes specific areas such as budgeting or scheduling. Al does not interfere in the areas assigned. An assistant notes, "He delegates with the clear expectation that it will get done. He promotes ownership but is behind the scenes."

His most frequently used "behind the scenes" technique is to listen, offer advice, consult, share information, and start informal dialogue. At the end of one school day, Al met with a teacher in preparation for a school board presentation. He followed her lead in the discussion, listening attentively, nodding, and offering reassurance or reinforcement. Occasionally, he embellished a thought by adding an idea or detail, all the while taking notes. When the presentation was solidified, Al concluded with an encouraging, enthusiastic approval. "Do it!" he said. "You give the information you're comfortable with. I'll fill in." Al gives priority to people, not policy, and is unafraid to bend or challenge rules when necessary.

Most of the responsibility for routine work and curriculum development is delegated to department heads and their staff members. Al organizes occasional department head meetings, releasing teachers for a half day or a full day so they have time to "share and discuss." "Usually, we meet at 7:30 a.m. and pass out information. In the full-day session we had time to speak our piece. I felt the camaraderie; we talked about integrating the curriculum." Al concurs: "You need the time to sit down with a manageable number of folks where you can exchange ideas. They enjoyed the time together and being brought on board." Generous time during the school day contributes to department sharing. "We get as much department head time as we want. He allows flexibility in scheduling or provides substitutes so we can do curriculum development."

Al encourages department heads to play a linking role from their staff members to the principal. "Twenty microscopes were broken and I took the problem to Al," relates one department head. "He got $1,000 to fix them." "Department heads play a big role in carrying concerns to the principal and act as an intermediary between Al and the department." A lot of power and decision making is still centered with department heads, but, as Al notes, "We don't have a lot of meetings because we don't have to." Al uses department heads for some of the operational, repetitive tasks. Ad hoc groups are formed to handle the unique, such as the proposal for "Schools for the 21st Century," a competitive state grant.[1]

The staff has been interested in cross-department sharing and building time into the school day for staff development. A proposal developed for the 21st Century grant reflects the vision. The development of the proposal began when Al heard about the legislation. He began explaining the legislation in "small doses at faculty meetings" and informally. You "gotta plant seeds and keep watering 'em," Al says. He approached teachers but didn't seek anyone in particular to serve on the planning committee. Some volunteered to work on the proposal, and eventually a group of seven or eight people became the core organizing and planning group. Participation by the others varied because he "always left the process open to anyone."

The proposal became a vehicle for the whole school to continue growth, challenge, and new learning. It was as though the previous six years of work with the reform movement had been pulled together, and the proposal acted as a catalyst. Al sees the proposal "as a vehicle to get to where we're going to get sooner." The ideas in the proposal represent the involvement of many, over time, and there is a consensus that, if the proposal is not funded, "we'll do it anyway." Al's handiwork is noticeable in the whole process. He had the idea and "pulled the faculty along." Everyone

---

[1]Grants were to be awarded to 21 innovative schools for whom all state rules and regulations would be waived.

is aware of the importance of the 21st Century proposal, and students relate with pride that he wanted their input. Al presented the 21st Century proposal to the ASB and "got real excited and enthusiastic about it," a contrast to his normally calm demeanor. "He likes new things and I think he believes you've got to change to grow," said another student.

After continual adjustment to "iron out the wrinkles," the original 2-page set of ideas blossomed into a 30-page document. A few staff members were concerned that the proposal would mean just more meeting time. But after discussions with individuals to determine if objections could be accommodated, the final vote was unanimous approval of the proposal.

Al has worked to develop a climate of support and trust at his school, while simultaneously planting seeds for new ideas. "He's a lot different from anybody I ever worked with. He has so much trust and faith that you won't let him down. There's a lot of things I don't agree with him on, but it's easy to do a good job because he expects it."

A Strong Captain, a Seasoned Crew

As you descend the short, spiral driveway leading to the parking lot, the substantial size of this high school is apparent. The street level, elevated in terraced fashion above the parking lots, rises significantly above the roof tops of the school buildings. The school is nestled in an area of heavy traffic, and location is a weakness noted by students who describe the campus as unattractive and "in a gully." A short walk down a steep concrete stairway takes the visitor to a building marked "Administration Office." This terraced descent is symbolic of a physical and mental depar-ture from the "outside world." The neatness of the campus grounds is impressive, and the brightly blooming spring flowers are evidence of the principal's specific efforts to improve the school's appearance. But as the 1,420 students converge in the hallways, "people get careless with trash" and litter becomes a problem. Custodians work on the school grounds throughout the day. On her way down the hall, the principal often stops to pick up paper, a pop can, or other refuse, which she promptly deposits in a nearby receptacle. "She's trying very hard to keep the campus neat," says one parent.

Jan, the principal, has been in this position for six years. However, she has influenced the school since its opening. She taught here at the beginning of her career 24 years ago and later became science department head. Visitors are impressed by Jan's businesslike demeanor, exemplified by her gray suit, white shirt, and necktie. Her rational approach to school management is evident throughout her daily activities. She emphasizes, for example, gathering complete and thorough data before making decisions.

"Getting data is the real key; that's the physicist in me. . . . The best decisions are made with the most data."

Her educational beliefs are well articulated and permeate the organization. From the beginning of her tenure, she made it clear that professional growth is expected from all. She places a strong emphasis on improvement of instruction and staff development. Teachers should "be better at the end of this year than last, and I want that reflected in instruction skills, not in cleaner files." There is no question who is in charge of learning at this school. Teacher observations occur more frequently than required by law. Department heads, trained in clinical supervision, observe teachers twice yearly, in addition to two observations by one of the three administrators. Jan focuses her energies on "evaluating teachers and designing proactive improvement programs." The assistant principals are "very good at managing the school" for the day-to-day operations such as scheduling, attendance, and student activities. "I don't do much of that these days," she reports.

Improvement is a full-time, never-ending job. "You'll see us always working on something." Teachers have yearly goals, overall school goals, and department goals. The staff was involved in a self-study in 1988 that focused on the development of a proposal for the Schools for the 21st Century grant. Growth is "energizing" to Jan, and she repeatedly conveys this vision to staff and community. "I say things that create moods, like 'We're simply the best; we're committed to excellence.' It is interesting how these statements show up throughout the year and for years to come," she said.

Her no-nonsense, "tight-ship" approach punctuates the interview. Jan is a self-described "strong leader." "I know how I want the school to be run. But I learned a long time ago you can't just impose that on people." Her need to drive the staff and her realization that change occurs slowly are philosophies she continually juggles. Waiting does not come easily to this advocate of change. She imagines an earlier time when a leader could impose decisions unchallenged and notes that patience is an attribute she has had to learn. For example, during the last two years, greater skills in reaching consensus have been required because of a new agreement that empowers teachers through school decision-making councils. Helping staff members make decisions for themselves has rewarded her practiced patience. "It works," she says. "As impatient as I get with it, we do make better decisions."

A sense of control and desire to be on top of everything is evident in every detail, including her choice of office location. The offices tucked in the back of the administrative wing are more prestigious and spacious, with room for amenities such as a conference table. The office Jan selected is small and unassuming but lies directly outside an office area where few activities escape her notice. Her door is almost always open as an invitation to drop-ins, but also as a way to monitor problems as they develop.

Recognized as a sincere, caring, and efficient principal, she commands the respect of the staff and parents for her tireless efforts. "She doesn't know what her house looks like. It's not a 9-to-5 job with her." She is described as a dedicated, hard worker, and her office lights are often seen "burning late into the night." Some worry that she tries to do too much or keep too many things going at the same time. Currently completing a doctorate at the University of Washington, Jan is aware of the implications of a demanding schedule. "I have to keep myself well, too; I work weeks on end without a break; that includes weekends." High expectations, most rigorously imposed on herself, mitigate what sometimes seems to be her lack of patience with the slowness of change. Compared to other principals, her time and involvement in district and state activities is seen as very extensive. Her political clout is admired.

Although the staff is strong, morale is reportedly low. Declining enrollment has resulted in three years of surplusing teachers, and those remaining have received only one minor raise in the past three years. "There's some crankiness here," which is a source of distress to a principal bent on change, growth, and improvement. A teacher-drawn cartoon placed on the faculty room bulletin board captures a frequently expressed sentiment. It shows teachers standing in the cafeteria line: "What are you gonna do with your salary increase?" the first asks. "I thought I might have the Jello," responds the second.

Despite the problems, parents recognize this as an outstanding school with an outstanding principal because of her leadership, example, and drive. "She pushes you, and maybe the staff sees her as a tough cookie, but I like that in a person." Parents support Jan and realize that a principal would have to be a strong and skillful leader to influence a staff resistant to new ideas. The maturity of this staff is striking. Fifty-eight of the 70 teachers have taught for 20 or more years, and 28 of them have logged more than 25 years in teaching. These teachers view themselves as knowledgeable professionals, strong and experienced.

At the end of the student day, the principal begins her toughest work. The Faculty Senate meets twice monthly, and this day budget proposals are scheduled for review. Now Jan's image relaxes; the jacket and tie are tossed aside and replaced by a casual open neck and rolled-up sleeves. The signal is clear: this is a working meeting. The school's district has a history of support for school-centered decision making and a process approach to problem solving. Staff consensus and participation in decision making is required by the collective bargaining agreement, but it is also a value of the school. The formation of a site council with "real" decision-making power has required new skills of principals. A shift from advising to decision making has changed the tone of staff-principal interaction, and principals are expected to be "more proficient at making decisions by consensus." Trial and error and numerous teacher-principal interactions are shaping new roles, working them out in daily practice.

The department heads, administrators, the secretary representing classified staff, and four teachers elected at-large assemble in the home economics room for the senate meeting. A parent, normally in attendance, is absent. The desks are arranged in a square to allow face-to-face dialogue. Jan has provided coffee, and she returns from the cafeteria with a container of almond cookies. These little touches are appreciated by a tired staff not looking forward to a budget battle. "Organized and efficient," Jan has prepared all of the necessary data to begin the discussion. A worksheet divided by columns lists each department's last allocation, the amount remaining, and this year's request. Going alphabetically by department, each spokesperson reviews an itemized request and explains the justification for the amount so "we understand them all." Several teachers indicate items they could voluntarily cut. However, requests still total $30,000, and more cuts must be made. Questions and conversations are surprisingly cordial, and laughter occasionally fills the room over requests like "teeny beepers" for the library. During the dialogue, the science department head sits by a computer and deletes agreed-upon items. The current balance occasionally is reported as the staff strives for a balanced budget. Suggestions and alternatives to requests are offered by others, and sometimes the principal volunteers "to scrounge around" and find something that could replace a purchase. Yet one continually senses that the principal is in control. Few harsh words are allowed and reports proceed without incident. Jan is purposefully "aggressive at managing the process" and feels strongly that it cannot work unless "people behave themselves." Although some view this control as a lack of openness to dissension, it is "not Jan's style to let people get on each other," reports an appreciative teacher. "Colleagues fighting" is a repugnant thought.

Almost two hours later, the last department reviews items, and total requests still exceed the available budget by $15,000. "I don't know what else we can do as a group," Jan states, and she indicates she will do some "individual negotiating" with teachers to see if other items can be deleted. No one disagrees and many seem happy to relinquish the final decision and leave school life behind for the day. The senate members nod in agreement or remain silent as Jan reminds them that this is "what we've been doing for a few years."

"Jan's pretty sharp," offers one observer. The staff is not in open "rebellion against the administration," as in other places. Jan would probably agree. "I've been doing this awhile and I'm halfway good at it. People who are fairly good move on by now. This is what I like to do so I stick with it." Not everyone would choose to be a high school principal with its multiple demands and diverse pulls of a strong staff. Jan likes the challenge.

The next two portraits describe middle/junior high school principals who are instructional leaders. As you read the portrait of Bob in "Good Communicator," you sense that in many ways he is more like Jan in "Strong Captain" than like Al in "A Seed-Planting Viking." Bob is aggressive, demanding, and data driven. The principal from "A Leader of Complex Transition," Sally, is an articulate, skilled expert in human relations. Clearly, Bob is running a school that, for the most part, is "in place," and he is a good example of consistency in instructional leadership over time. Sally, on the other hand, is a good example of the trials and tribulations of a strong instructional leader guiding a reluctant staff from the routines of a traditional junior high school to a new, child-centered middle school.

A Good Communicator

Located in a comfortable Seattle suburb, this junior high has a cluster of buildings, campus style, to serve its student body of around 700. At the hub is the administration building. The principal, Bob, was well prepared for our visit, with staff and student interviews scheduled for the day.

As we talked, Bob described how he was brought in to "shape things up" in a school he characterized as "a country club." Students spent their days partying in the woods next to the school, drug problems were severe, and teachers arrived late for their classes and "beat the kids out of the parking lot."

Bob changed all that—and quickly. He met first with parents. As a new principal, he held 16 parent meetings, visited homes, used a questionnaire, talked, and took notes. He individually interviewed teachers. He then provided the information he gathered to the staff in planning changes in the school. At a staff meeting he presented his philosophy for the school.

At the end of three years, with the help of staff and parents, this junior high was a changed school, its staff imbued with a pioneer spirit. The next challenge Bob met was to improve the curriculum, and he worked with staff members in response to suggestions from John Goodlad. Teachers report that Bob has been a powerful force as an instructional leader, committed to spending time in the classroom helping teachers with their instruction.

As he spoke of his school, Bob discussed the need for control—how things had been out of control when he took over and how he had achieved control. But on the wall of his office are framed color photos of quiet, charming one-room country schoolhouses in Pennsylvania, Nebraska, and Montana, which his mother collected for him on her travels throughout the U.S. This unspoken quality displayed on the wall, caring for others, is apparent in the way that members of the staff speak about each other and about Bob.

Bob's staff describes him as forceful, honest, up-front—the authority who makes the final decision. At the same time, they speak of the trust he places in them, his support and encouragement of their ideas, and how highly they value their autonomy as teachers. Bob did not speak of the harmony within departments, or how he encourages positive interpersonal staff relationships, but his staff did. Complementary traits seemed to be balanced in his leadership.

A teacher in the lunchroom said, "Bob has the ability to start the year with a plan, and all year long you know the decisions he makes will be focused on that plan." He works with the staff, collectively; develops a plan; and communicates it. He is decisive and makes the plan happen. In this organized, orderly school, respect, an old-fashioned virtue, is key, and it is everywhere—in the kitchen and in the attitudes of the secretaries and the students. This school is very different from other schools that the staff has been in. Here, it is like a family.

According to his secretary, Bob uses two decision-making processes: an immediate, decisive response when he must, or getting all the facts together and organizing them, which he much prefers. His secretary says he is much happier when he has all the facts when he is making a decision. For example, in looking over interview information for a new secretary, he organized all the information on a chart with point values.

Staff-initiated and developed curriculum has spread from the school throughout the district and further. Bob expects, encourages, and supports excellence in teaching. Teachers report that Bob is an expert evaluator and has helped them improve their teaching. Current goals for school improvement are centered on curriculum and instruction, based on the recommendations made by John Goodlad. Teacher leadership surfaces; teachers are excited about teaching and come early and stay late. The staff describes curriculum development as being initiated by teachers and supported by their principal. Bob tells them, "Go for it."

"We have a good staff here." "He has confidence in the staff." "In other schools, the staff is dead." Again and again, coworkers commended each other. High standards and good judgment are seen in how Bob selects varied, talented, and hardworking people for the staff.

The staff is not expected to be concerned with details of nonteaching activities. Duties for lunch are taken care of by the principal and the vice principal. A stipend pays the supervisor of the lunchtime activity room. Orderly procedures for student discipline are followed. Teachers are expected to monitor the students as they move from class to class and keep an eye on those in the classroom.

Students have access to the adults. One articulate student got the librarian's attention: "Karl, what is it?" asked the librarian. "I need to talk to you, I'm really angry," said the child. "Okay, just give me 10 minutes," answered the librarian, who later took a few minutes to talk with the student privately. An aide emphasizes that caring about kids is what really matters in this school. Many staff members believe Bob finds teachers who are fine people, with diverse interests, whose philosophy is caring about the kids.

The expectation at this school is that students who have problems will be heard by the counselors and that the counselors will work with students on a decision. That decision may not be what individual students want but what is best for them in the eyes of the adult.

The students interviewed (ranging from special education to honors students) spoke of the importance of education in their lives. They saw a good, strong basic education as a necessity for opportunities and choices in the future. Although students seemed unaware of what the principal did, one certainly expressed confidence in that authority as he told Bob, "I told that fellow about all the neat things you do; now will you buy me lunch?"

Students get along with each other very well. An 8th grader mentioned that she formed strong friendships in her 7th grade core program. Students appear busy, spirited, and polite. Students and parents say discipline is good, fair, and equitable. "My son was required to stay after school for a behavior problem in class. When he got home, he had resolved it, understood it, said that he was fairly treated, and that he was at fault."

Parents were brought into school decisions by the principal as soon as he began. Strong connections are maintained with Tuesday morning coffees. The secretary sends out personal invitations so that during the year every parent is invited to one of the Tuesday coffees with Bob. Parents are involved in curriculum committees and are volunteers in the school. Teachers are expected to communicate with parents about student problems, and they do.

Students, parents, and the new assistant principal all said that if there was one thing to export from their school, it was good communication. According to the secretary, Bob never refuses to take or return a phone call from a parent. His door is always open to the staff. Bob is very capable in communicating on all levels—with the staff, parents, and students. The staff notes that he communicates clearly, and his message is strong. He manages communication by scheduling an appropriate number of meetings and frequent get-togethers.

The staff also says that communication is a two-way process. If a staff member is unhappy about another staff member, or disagrees with Bob, that person can go into Bob's office and talk it over for a fair hearing and a good exchange of information. In the same way that Bob is always available for parents, he is also available to the staff. Staff members said that when a teacher grumbles about Bob, it is the teacher's problem. "The teacher should see Bob and resolve it."

By self-report, Bob feels that he is not sensitive enough. One staff member stated that he is "not as humanistic as people want him to be." Yet many gave examples of very humane and sensitive actions. For example, in an evaluation he said, "You've done a very good job helping someone else out who's been grieving." How Bob knew of this action was a mystery to the staff member. Bob encouraged peer support and financial support for another teacher in a stressful family situation. Teachers report him as being very perceptive in knowing what is going on in a teacher's classroom and an expert in providing evaluation.

He also gets high marks for his treatment of women and minorities, although it is not entirely natural. He pays attention to it. Aides, often the underclass in a school, are well treated. One aide commented, "In this school, my needs are respected equally with teachers'." Although the socioeconomic make-up of the student population is fairly homogeneous, cultural diversity of students is celebrated in a curriculum program. The staff perceives his vision as including the "best education for each individual." Commenting on positive results for all students in the core program, Bob said, "We've learned that 'giftedness' can be how you act on students."

In any group of people, some have the principal's ear more than others, but politics was barely mentioned in Bob's school.

Several staff members mentioned the changing orientation of society, from the permissiveness of the 1970s to emphasis on school improvement of the 1980s. The staff finds this "tight ship" with "taut control" a very easy place to teach and to focus on excellence. To a degree, the school reflects the community and changing context from the '70s to the '80s. Parents say this school has become a neat place for kids.

Now in quieter waters, will the veteran teachers keep their sense of mission? As new staff members enter into this work group, unaware of past struggles and successes, will they buy into the high norms that exist? Will something else be needed to reward a hardworking staff? Perhaps there will not be that fire and spirit expressed by those on the staff who had been involved in the metamorphosis into an orderly school that meets high expectations.

Also, financial resources are currently diminishing. A grant provided extra planning time for the core teams, but that money is no longer available, and neither is the planning time. The staff felt that its teaching as well had been diminished. Since "Bob doesn't rest on his laurels," what is next for the school?

"Bob intends to make the school the best junior high in the country," said one staff member. Bob is proud of the positive results of the core program on student achievement and teacher morale and speaks of manipulating time to fit instruction. Teachers describe each other as "outstanding." The P.E. teacher proudly describes the "no cuts" sports program that enables all students to participate in sports. Whatever else happens, this school represents important educational values. The structure and the order support a strong academic program. The bottom line is that the child is first, and staff members work together toward what is best for the student.

A Leader of Complex Transition

Articulate and skilled in human relations, Sally began her principalship at the middle school two years ago. The school had postponed serious attention to the districtwide commitment to change from a junior high to middle school concept until she arrived. As a result, Sally inherited a situation that was full of potential stress for staff members, students, and community. The tension revolved around the different philosophies of a middle school concept and traditional secondary schools. This is clearly a school in the throes of complex transition. Some frustrated teachers wanted to continue to teach secondary content; now they were asked to "teach the kids rather than the subject." The changes include a switch from a six- to a seven-period day to add an advisory period for students, instruction in blocks of time, and exploratory classes for 6th graders. These adjustments have demanded flexibility and cooperation on the part of the whole staff. Sally believes that a good leader "has to be truly involved in what's going on," and she is.

In spite of the considerable stress created by this stepped-up transition to a middle school, Sally has maintained a strong sense of direction and continually works to facilitate change and growth. She believes that all staff members "need to be examples to children," and she holds them and herself accountable for doing what is right for children in their classrooms. Progress toward the middle school concept is slow, but evidence of change can be seen this year as "people are talking more about educational issues." She is an "idea champion" who rewards innovation, creativity, and different ways of thinking and knowing. Sally's vision is a staff committed to creating an environment where all students learn. Teaching should be designed to give students "tools to use in a flexible, fast-changing environment." The chemistry of the teachers and children in the classroom is the key to making this vision work. Sally would like to see the atmosphere relaxed, with the focus on teaching children how to access information, how to learn, and how to enjoy learning. The vision for the school is a community where people care for each other, enjoy learning together, and share in mutual roles of good citizenship.

The staff is organized in teams for interdisciplinary instruction. Initially, some teachers would not cooperate with the team concept. Sally was "not willing to have people say 'I don't want to be on a team.' " She notices this year that teachers are more apt to "get into each other's classrooms and share." Certain teams are operating "in name only," and both Sally and the teachers involved recognize the need to grow in skills of working together toward a consensus model. Next year it will be more possible to team teach since the staff has "created common planning periods." Sally recognizes the need to restructure the day to encourage people to work together. "If you don't provide time within the workday, it doesn't happen."

Sally's involvement extends to the classroom. She believes a good principal "needs to keep involved." Sally would like to be in "several classrooms every day," and she is disappointed that she has not been able to assist in instruction that much this year. She "likes to take over in classrooms," and she does not arrange a substitute for short periods when teachers need to be out of the building. These situations provide her the opportunity to continue teaching. Throughout the school, high expectations are held for student learning; kids know that teachers expect them to "do our homework and [they] want us to learn."

The team approach to decision making and program planning is evident throughout the operational plan. A Program Improvement Council consists of 10 team leaders and 2 instructional facilitators. When the problems of logistics and mechanics are resolved, Sally's goal is to talk with this group about improving the overall school. Ever hopeful, Sally feels that "the potential is great, but we've barely scratched the surface." Teams are also extended to student input in decision making. The Student Senate has representatives from each grade level and a faculty advisor. They control the Associated Student Body funds, which this year are considerable. When we visited, they were deliberating about the precedent they will set if they pay for the full amount of the 8th grade field trip and which animal they should sponsor for the zoo. Each request for funding is decided by the students at this meeting.

Parents sit on the Program Improvement Council, and the PTSA is being shaped into an active group. Sally notes that the process of getting parents involved is "a struggling, growing thing." A spaghetti dinner and talent show with 550 people took place a few weeks ago, and Sally laughs about the progress. "Junior high kids aren't noted for wanting their parents involved in school." Yet the need for a growing, active school-community partnership is another goal Sally will pursue.

Sally is a human relations and counseling expert, and her concern for people and their needs is evident in her decision-making style. Her office door is open, and she is always available. Her office is decorated with things adult and things friendly to adolescents (books, dragons, ducks, stuffed animals, family pictures, and toys). The physical plant is designed in clusters, and classroom space is spread out. Teachers are not conveniently close to their grade-level team. Sally's concern for human needs prompted her not to move two teachers who will retire this year. Next year, these classrooms will be moved to facilitate team planning and teaching. The most stressful part of this year has been the change to seven periods. Sally had to work to integrate secondary teachers used to operating "on a 55-minute clinical hour" and elementary teachers who think "not having the kids all day is terrible." With empathy, Sally notes that these teachers have "been doing it 20 years and it's difficult to change." In the short term, change will take longer to accomplish; in the long run, she hopes that her patience will gain her the respect and commitment of her staff.

Sally recognizes that change takes time. She sees her role as a facilitator in the process. The transition to the middle school concept was difficult, and Sally and the staff learned a great deal in the process. Sally recalls, "I expected too much; I expected people to become more kid-oriented by virtue of the fact that we changed to a middle school." Sally's understanding of the magnitude of the changes and growth that staff members have made help her maintain patience with the process. "They didn't know there was a difference in young adolescence," she said. Before her transfer to this school, Sally was able to fill the facilitator role at another school that made a smooth transition to the middle school concept. She reminisces about the thorough planning process she helped develop. "We had visits to middle schools, inservice, and workshops; the staff was ready." On the other hand, at this school the transition had to be accomplished in only one year. Sally feels that people "need time in between [inservice] to talk about how it would be for them, how it would work."

The major strength of the school is the teaching staff, which consists of "strong people; I'd stack them up against any staff." The school has the "potential to be a first-class middle school." Transition will take three to five years to complete.

The challenge of communication between more than 60 adults in and around the building is a concern. Sally takes personal responsibility for letting everyone know what is going on. Teachers talk about Sally as "a great listener . . . she gets back to everyone." The difficult transition was complicated by small groups of teachers who had a sense of territory and control. Sally has confronted these problems directly through visible, active communication. Teachers find her "open to new ideas within the organization." She actively seeks input and considers their suggestions; she supports their growth. Sally "plants little seeds and lets people contribute." As an example, teachers note her willingness to discuss and modify the advisory period. Teachers want input in the future to clarify the ambiguity of school goals and to have time to plan ahead. Some are also hopeful that the school can "be rid of troublemakers [certain teachers]."

The student population is 17 percent minority, and 20 percent of students receive free lunch. Sally advocates the best possible education for all students. Tracking practices that have been standard in the past are changing. "We don't believe in it here," remarks Sally. "The staff and I are struggling to change it." However, the itinerant music teacher's schedule makes the total elimination of tracking problematic because it forces students into inflexible groups. A gifted program is also a future target for change, even though the "instruction is really great." Sally recalls being "nebulous on purpose" about the program and its goals since she does not believe in self-contained gifted programs. Pressure from parents and the central office to maintain programs for gifted children has slowed change in that area. The school has, in another building, an extensive program that serves the needs of a variety of developmentally delayed and physically handicapped youngsters. Sally points out a classroom directly across the courtyard from her office and talks about her future plans. "I want to move these classrooms [special education] right down here; I'm in the process of making that happen." The whole building has been made handicapped-accessible to make this change possible. Why is Sally such an advocate? "It's good for everyone not to separate these kids. We miss opportunities by not involving ourselves directly in the education of handicapped students." The final goal is to have all kids perceive themselves not as special education kids or gifted kids, but as kids.

The whole staff is responsible for providing a safe, caring, and enjoyable learning environment for all kids. Sally has brought order and control. Before she came, the school had problems with student attitude, behavior, and vandalism, yet it was considered one of the top academic schools in the city. Perhaps the ultimate question about the well-being of a school is: Would you send your child here? One of the teachers remarks that this school is a "safe place for kids—I'd send my child here." The year before Sally came, the highest rate of vandalism in the city was at this school; this has changed. A parent sees the students as calmer this year. "Drinking and drugs have been cleared up." Although school discipline is improving, there is need for consistency and strengthening in this area. The assistant principal handles most of the problems now, but Sally is visible to the students, she knows the children's names, and she is "right on top of it." Students like and respect her. They say, "She helps us, she smiles a lot, and she knows me." Students are given room "to be kids," and there is a sense of joking and fun in their lunchroom conversations. Yet Sally quickly ushers into her office two students (suspended from another school) who are "visiting their friends." Parents are contacted, the principal of the other school is notified, and the girls are picked up and sent home. There is no doubt about the limits to which fun is allowed in this building.

Sally is able to capitalize on the special talents of the staff. Master teachers are high quality, and teachers feel they "do well academically." There is a shared sense of respect between the staff and the administration. One teacher remarked, "It's nice to be respected and trusted," and another said, "Sally trusts my judgment." Sally knows her staff works hard and shows her respect in many ways. She gave them a surprise break by scheduling a longer lunch period, and she shows small signs of appreciation. Sally feels that she is "successful at attracting teachers and maintaining them." Several teachers asked to be transferred to this school because they had worked previously with Sally and wanted to continue. "She's the best I've ever worked with." Sally is seen by teachers as key in making the transition to the middle school happen against great odds. Clearly, the philosophy, which is shared by most of the staff, and the details of building a middle school that is designed for student needs are still evolving. Those teachers perceived as "not liking kids" will have to be transferred, or adapt, if the whole school is to succeed.

At the end of the day, Sally worries about the girl who took a bottle and a half of aspirin during period three. She plans to visit her at the hospital on the way home. No doubt she will also be worrying about scheduling and the fast pace for students and teachers. Also on that worry list will be how to get time in the schedule—time for shared planning, for clarifying goals, for enjoyment of kids and each other, and for reflection. This school is not a tidy example of a school where everything is running smoothly; this is a school in the throes of transition. Sally is keenly aware of the complexities and is able to lead the transition. She is a "growth person" and promotes the learning of others. Sally knows she does not have all the answers; she enjoys the give and take of professional relationships and feels she can learn a lot from the mentor principal experience. This middle school, under Sally's leadership, will make an excellent site for a strong intern who wants to learn about how to influence change in complex environments. Sally did not have the opportunity to work with a strong principal while she was learning to be an administrator. "I feel I have a responsibility to give back to the profession."

We have chosen three schools to illustrate instructional leadership at the elementary level. The portrait of Bonnie in "Double Enrichment" presents the elementary principal as a fearless leader who at the same time is seen by outsiders as shy, humble, yet indomitable in spirit. Bonnie is a principal in a large urban elementary school. On the other hand, Del, in "Problems and Opportunities," operates an elementary school in a fast-growing suburban district, and Dana, in "A Soft Touch of Well-Being," operates an elementary school in a medium-sized Western town—a town fast growing into a multifaceted city. All display quite different styles—from Bonnie's fearless leadership to Dana's soft touch. All clearly provide the leadership necessary to focus their school on curriculum and instructional issues.

Double Enrichment

This elementary school is a large, remodeled structure with a busy freeway on one side and neighborhood homes on the other. This was a school that the district considered closing in 1982. No one—principals, teachers, or students—wanted to go there. When Bonnie became principal, it became a magnet school to assist in the district's voluntary desegregation plan. It has expanded from less than 200 mostly minority students to a richly diverse population of 550 students in grades K-5, with a long waiting list for the 1988-89 school year. The school offers a variety of special programs to attract students. The LEAP program for autistic and regular preschoolers is one of a kind. The Therapeutic Learning Center, which "other schools in the district didn't want to take," is offered as well as a computer lab, the Writing to Read Program, curriculum integration, the Home Helpers Program, and several others. It is clear that the school philosophy is a "commitment to quality."

Bonnie is the "fearless leader." Born and reared in India, she proudly wears her native costume. She provides a fascinating study of leadership with influences from both Eastern and Western cultures. In her office is a large banner entitled "Fearless Leader," a poem, and a variety of gifts presented to her by the staff for "Bosses' Week." Joy, the main office secretary who has been with Bonnie since 1982, interrupts our discussion to tell Bonnie that she "simply must attend the faculty breakfast" since it is in her honor. The faculty breakfast is a frequent event giving staff members a chance to socialize informally. Bonnie seldom takes time for socializing in her busy schedule, with a staff of 64 people and no assistant principal. She is at the same time shy, humble, and indomitable. The school runs well because she has become a master at recognizing and putting the talents of others to work to assist in the instruction and leadership of the school. The staff clearly recognizes and respects her high expectations, her strong leadership, and her vision.

Bonnie has a reputation for high expectations of the staff and the students. A parent whose children have attended more than 12 different schools in the district finds this school "different because they push the kids to learn. There are lots of opportunities for kids." Teachers acknowledge that Bonnie expects "something from all of us." The school's reputation is clear in the district: "You don't go there unless you want to work hard." Bonnie and the teachers are "extremely hardworking." Bonnie is credited by one teacher for "molding the school." "Resourceful" and "painfully direct," Bonnie has a clear vision of what she wants and goes after it at all levels within the system. Some say the central office staff hate to see her coming because she refuses to take no for an answer. "She really motivates people," are the words of one teacher who proudly says, "I am an excellent teacher now, and it's because of Bonnie." Another teacher remembers the painful days when Bonnie first began as principal, "Everyone was crazy; she was in the classroom all the time!"

One of Bonnie's goals for the school is to retrain teachers for better schools in the future. This strong push for achievement is present everywhere. In the words of one teacher, "You have to grow here." The teachers share the desire to find ways to raise the achievement of students by raising the level of expectation. An outcome of high expectations is visible in improved achievement scores. Bonnie and the reading specialist review the scores on the district Specific Learning Objectives Test used in the school district and celebrate the fact that 80 percent of the students in the 3rd grade achieved mastery. Another grade level appeared to need some work; Bonnie made the personal commitment to look into the reasons and make plans for improvement. "If the kids are not performing, I ask what's wrong." This year the goal of "all 1st graders reading on grade level" resulted in the improvement in the number of sight words children were able to read. Bonnie finds this gain "remarkable for us" and anticipates that by 3rd grade, the goal will be met for most of these children. "A school that serves underprivileged kids needs to be doubly enriched, because they [students] don't get it anywhere else." Bonnie's statement speaks clearly of the commitment to quality and excellence in educational opportunity that permeates the building.

"This school is a shining star . . . ; kids will go into the next century with the skills they need," proudly comments a 4th grade teacher. The school was selected in a state competition for "Schools for the 21st Century." The proposal was written by a group of volunteer teachers. Originally the idea was Bonnie's, but she "didn't want to push it." Before the team of writers would submit the proposal, they insisted that everyone in the building agree to the plan. Now the impression among staff is that "everyone loves it [the proposal]." Parent education, community involvement, redefinitions of community, curriculum, and presentation of materials are the themes of the proposal. Bonnie's vision is of a school that is "flexible" and "sees the need to change" and has a commitment to provide children with the skills to compete that increase self-concept. These are overriding principles of the future goals. Bonnie wants to help children succeed, but not by force; further implied is the need for children to "enjoy learning." Bonnie's schooling in a different education system strengthens and shapes her commitment to help her students succeed in a competitive world.

The school operates so smoothly and calmly one would hardly suspect the breadth of special programs within its walls. The complexity of this magnet school and the extent of its programs are at first somewhat overwhelming. The school is organized around three themes: Science and Math, Global Studies, and Positive Climate. Handbooks full of integrated interdisciplinary instructional ideas and units have been developed by the teachers. Each month a theme is chosen and emphasized throughout the school. The science and math theme during our visit was "Animals"; the Global Studies theme was "Asia"; and Positive Climate was emphasized by the phrase, "Plant a Seed of Kindness." The classrooms and halls are fascinating children's museums. Around the school we saw charts and children-made murals of exotic butterflies, endangered species, the sea life chain, a map of the Northwest Trek, whales, and a wall mural of the reed meadow showing hatching ducks and other birds.

In addition to curriculum involvement, the whole staff looks at behavior in terms of "preventive discipline." Several staff members volunteered to work together for several weeks of the summer to write a discipline handbook based on the logical-consequences model authored by Dreikurs. Several teachers assist on the playground before school begins, and four others ride the buses at the beginning of the year to help establish the routine and prevent problems. Bonnie walks the halls as students come into the school, greeting and encouraging them, stopping problems as they come up. Every time students leave the classrooms in groups, they are escorted by an adult in orderly fashion to lunch, to the library, and to other special programs.

Bonnie believes that "very consistent, tight control" eliminates most of the discipline problems you might expect in a school with a population as diverse as this one. A positive approach to managing learning and behavior is essential to Bonnie. "I really emphasize positive attitude. I do not yell at kids and I do not expect others to." When the school became a magnet school, "teachers knew we were going to become this big school and they wanted to do it well and have a plan. . . . We emphasize the positive." Each teacher is expected to have a classroom discipline plan. Bonnie emphasizes that part of the discipline plan is the very close supervision of children. Bonnie believes that "as a problem starts, you can stop it." In the classrooms with the emphasis on achievement, there is active, creative learning going on. Bonnie remarks that in well-taught classrooms, children are "just too busy; there's too much happening for problems."

Bonnie has seen only six students this year for discipline problems. Teachers take care of their own discipline concerns. On the day of our site visit, one student was sent to the office for hitting another in the stomach. Very calmly, Bonnie helped this young girl work through the anger she felt, focusing the child with such questions as: "Who's in control of your temper? Who loses when you get angry in this way? What else could you have done?" Soon the girl is contentedly writing letters of apology to the other student and to her teacher.

"All children can learn" and "Learning takes many forms" are two prominent and interrelated themes. At a Student-of-the-Month Luncheon for parents and students, Bonnie conducts a discussion with the group on the meaning of citizenship. Good citizens are people who are "responsible, look for alternatives to solve problems, and obey the rules." "All kids should have opportunities"—this theme is evident throughout the school day. Those children selected as students of the month are not the standard class stars. They have been chosen for growth and improvement in things that are important to them as individuals. A bulletin board display with a color picture and a description of each student is found in the hall near the library. Similarly, the school extends opportunities to all students in academic areas. The school participates in the Young Authors program, which in most schools features a select number of children. Every child in Bonnie's school has written a book, which is displayed in the library and showcases in the halls. "Bonnie believes all kids can learn, and she believes in achievement . . . ; so do I," comments one of the 2nd grade teachers.

Everyone is involved in instruction at this school; few opportunities are missed to shape and influence the lives of these young citizens. We discover the custodian teaching a group of children about the electrical and heating system of the school, explaining what would happen if the lights went out.

Bonnie knows that teaching can be an isolated, lonely profession. She is concerned about breaking down that isolation and works to involve teachers in decisions about the school. The large staff includes over 64 people. If Bonnie were to individually meet the needs of each one, "they'd be lined up from 7:00 until 7:00 and only get five minutes, so I started a support group." The support group began by teachers nominating seven from their ranks to serve as support group members. The main function of the group was just to be available and listen. The group is now called the Rappers Problem Solving Team. Members are nominated by their peers, representing each special group within the school. The positions are staggered, so new members come on board every other year. This team now meets many needs, including school improvement, listening to teachers, prereferral for special services, and curriculum planning. There is an envelope in the main office for staff members to submit concerns they wish to bring up with the team. Bonnie feels that the group was necessary because of the change from a small school to a magnet school with many things going on. Bonnie is proud that this team "can help people feel a part of the building." The team is "really, really used," and teachers feel that it is "very beneficial" when questions are raised.

One wonders how Bonnie can influence the many activities in this busy, complex school. Bonnie feels her main influence is in the area of curriculum and instruction. "It is our focus; I want to provide the very best education for every child walking into this building." Bonnie is clear about her primary role. "I see myself as a teacher first; I know the problems that I faced and . . . if teachers want to do the best job they can, [I ask] 'How can I help each teacher be the best teacher he or she can be?' " Bonnie aims to set up a pyramid of relationships and influence. "I support teachers; teachers support each other; then they support kids." The choice to become a school administrator was based on the same principle. "I wanted to see if I could influence the whole school, not just the 30 kids in my classroom."

Bonnie also influences by modeling. "I am on task; I expect others to be on task." She adds, "Teachers should be professionals; I can't tell them what to do." But by modeling, Bonnie shapes part of this professional role. Teachers "do not have lunch and bus duty; I do those by myself." Yet during the fall, several teachers volunteered to ride the buses without pay. Bonnie feels that modeling is working to create a sense of professional responsibility. "They see me doing it for five years, and when I say I need help they come up with a solution; as a result we have fewer problems." Difficulties on bus rides is one of the biggest problems. There is inconsistency of drivers and thus inconsistency in expectations on the bus. Bonnie is concerned: "How can I expect the kids to behave when there is no consistency?"

What are the weaknesses in this school? Bonnie is comfortable in acknowledging that there will "always be weaknesses." There will always be "classrooms that need instructional improvement." Because the focal point of the school is curriculum and instruction, Bonnie feels that "it takes a lot of energy. Once we start, we cannot give up." An example of this ongoing energy toward improvement is seen in the writing program. Writing "has to be integrated into all subject areas. We cannot be satisfied if kids in 3rd grade cannot write a paragraph." Bonnie encourages giving "more meaningful homework" and suggests improvement in our "use of critical thinking." "Getting rid of dittos" is a technique Bonnie wishes to attempt to improve writing and thinking skills.

Bonnie keeps very involved in the school programs and in the broader community. She seldom misses learning opportunities and is eager to be involved with student interns from the Danforth Project. "From everyone I meet I learn something." She is aware that her tendency to be "very direct" can also create problems. Tempering directness by "preserving everyone's self-esteem" is one of Bonnie's personal improvement goals. She is also working to provide the positive feedback her teachers need for their hard work and successes. Bonnie recognizes that her own expectations are "extremely high," but she is committed to the whole staff establishing high expectations and motivating students to "enjoy learning." In promoting both high expectations and enjoyment of learning, Bonnie has found it necessary to work on accepting "people as they are."

This elementary school has a strong commitment to parents as partners in education. Bonnie knows "there's a lot to work on" and encourages their participation and support. Parents work as volunteers in the school, and there is a "fairly active" PTA. All subcommittees within the school decision-making structure have parent representatives on them. Teachers comment that parents "help with special events," including fund-raisers such as popcorn sales and the open house. The science fair and pizza party are to be held the evening of our visit. Parents are in the school helping set up the tables and displays, encouraging their children, and supporting the school. This school has a majority (90 percent) of students receiving free or reduced-price lunches. The growing involvement of parents is impressive. Bonnie works with the local community businesses to promote involvement in the school and to maintain positive relationships.

Bonnie never breaks her stride during this 12-hour day. While managing the science fair and pizza party, she is also concerned about improved expectations for writing and math for next year. This retraining will cost money, and she is prepared with grant support of $3,000. Bonnie is committed to allowing students to achieve, and she assists them by the way she organizes textbooks, materials, and instruction. Bonnie plans to use grant money to continue retraining teachers. The science fair is scheduled to follow the pizza party tonight. As another normal day for Bonnie heads into the evening, Bonnie is, as usual, "everywhere at once."

Problems are Opportunities

The approach to this elementary school is roundabout and somewhat confusing. Climbing the last hill, we see the school building only after we turn the last corner, and we experience part of what each student experiences every school day. All of the children arrive by bus; some ride as long as 45 minutes each day.

The school is in a modest glass and Roman brick, single-story building within the city limits of a growing urban area. The site has been leased by the school district for the past 10 years. Until recently it housed the overflow of students from a nearby area. This year, those students have moved to a new building, and now there is a new student body in an old building.

Del, the principal, greets the buses as they arrive every morning. He is a sturdy man of medium height, with calm blue eyes, short grayish-brown hair, and a ready smile. His healthy, unwrinkled skin and dimples belie the years of experience in which his leadership is firmly grounded. Del appears quietly and gently powerful. The small children he kneels to teach in a kindergarten class are attracted and soothed by his touch and his presence.

Asked, "What are you proud of about this school?" he tells how he and four other principals created plans for the school and presented them to the school board. He relates information about the beginnings of the school, the details of how student slots were allocated throughout the district, and recent changes in the rules. Del is proud of nearly everything about the school, including the older building, and perhaps even the shortage of supplies. He is especially proud of how well the school works and how much the kids love to be here. He can see advantages even where others might see liabilities.

Recently, parents have been pushing the school board to change the school's admission policies. Originally based on the first-come, first-served admission from the three basic areas of the district, parents are pushing for sibling preference. This sign of success presents a problem for Del, because it changes some basic tenets of the school and its situation. If admission is changed to sibling preference, half the kindergarten slots will be filled by siblings of current students. While this creates a supportive constituency for the school, it also means unequal access for students without siblings already enrolled.

Equity in education is important to Del and his view of important issues facing schools for the coming century. In addition, it may affect the "transfer effect" of practices in this school to other schools. Del wants the school to be seen as a "do-able model" for other schools. He believes strongly in the methods chosen for the school, which incorporate whole language, learning styles, and cooperative learning. The program structure facilitates a lower student/teacher ratio in core areas of reading and mathematics. Because of the economics of the busing situation, full-day kindergarten is used to address academic and social needs. Teachers rotate grade levels within primary and intermediate teams every two years. At-risk students benefit from heterogeneous learning groups that facilitate mainstreaming and promote equity for all students. They also represent application of the latest results of educational research, and Del says it is important that the school "represent the average student." He then explains, "Educators [are] very creative at making things fail; [they are] afraid to take risks." He finds it exciting to be at the cutting edge and says it's important to look at "common threads: look at the next century, the next decade." He states his belief that good education today must look to, and prepare students for, the future.

Del feels that he has "had lots of choices in life," probably more than most young people. His mother was a schoolteacher, and he feels an underlying commitment to serve people, especially young people. His reasons for not going to the central office include that it is "too far from the real action." While he could "make twice the money at Boeing," he is comfortable. His philosophy has been shaped by real life experiences, including struggles with "certain kinds of curricula." Every morning when he wakes up he knows he has the greatest job there is for him, and he thinks that "burn-out is a state of mind." From an early age, he wanted to be the best he could be, and since he is a building principal, he wants to do a good job. For him, the most important evaluation he faces every year is his own self-evaluation.

Del's two most important tasks for this day are to deal with a situation of unruly behavior by the 6th graders that is threatening a field trip to Victoria, British Columbia, and to eat lunch with the students at the table that showed the best lunchroom behavior for the month of March. In this school it is a very big deal to eat lunch with the principal.

Del organized and presented some of his concerns to the two classes of 6th graders about behavior expectations on a school-sponsored trip. He has prepared for the meeting carefully, his list of concerns has been typed, and he uses an overhead projector to present it to the students. His presentation is matter of fact, clear, and step-by-step. Del receives comments and questions from the students; he is attentive and his voice is calm and carefully controlled. He speaks more loudly a few times for emphasis, but he does not nag or whine at the students. He is very respectful and clear about his concerns, and he suggests to the students what they should think about and respond to in order to retain their special opportunities. They will have a few days to think about the situation and to formulate a response.

Del turns problems into opportunities. In his view, it is partly a matter of perception and partly a reflection of personal philosophy: Problems are negative and produce few winners, but if you can change a problem into an opportunity, then there are gains in the situation. This gentle confrontation with the 6th graders has given him a chance to get them to reflect on their responsibility for their own behavior and the choices they make for themselves. He talks about sharing feelings with students so that everyone has the same expectations and can share in solutions and responsible decisions.

The students talk about what is special about their school and about Del. "At our old school the principal was the boss. Here if the teacher has an idea, the principal takes the idea and tries to make a program. He's real understanding and kind. He's more approachable than some teachers." "He comes into a classroom and finds out about what other people are doing. The other principal just yelled at me and made me feel guilty. It seems like his voice is always down low." "He does stuff with kids. He holds kids' hands on the playground and talks. He always has enough time to throw a ball or say hello. He always has a smile. He doesn't get mad, and if he does get mad at the kids or the teachers, he just keeps it to himself."

Students liked voting on the school motto, the colors, the mascot, and the name Voyagers. They think most of the rules are appropriate and that some flexibility in interpretation is possible. Students liked the "Self-Management Award Party" for getting all their work in on time. They say, "We focus on math and reading—the way people learn here; we make it into a game. They teach us what it's going to be like in the real world. The other school just gave us worksheets. I like the teachers; they are new and young, and they do fun things. I think everybody's happy with our school." The students talk about Sharing Circle, where "we share our concerns." The specific rules state that group members cannot laugh at concerns, and they must listen. The Associated Student Body has a Supreme Court. "If kids feel they're not treated fairly, they can take it to the court. We write it up and give it to the principal, and he makes the final decision." The students can also take personal concerns to him. Del has learned that when you treat students with respect and give them appropriate guidelines, then you mainly have to "get out of their way." A self-described pragmatist, Del's years of experience have left him tuned in to staff needs. It is important to listen to their needs and who they are. With that knowledge he can encourage them to do their best work for each student.

A handmade red valentine heart on the wall of Del's office summarizes how his staff feels about him. "Dynamite leader, a real people person, impressive! Calming. A take charge kind of guy! Best boss I ever had; quietly dynamic! Supportive. Ability to make people feel comfortable. Never gets upset. Tops!" The unusual opportunity that Del had to pick his entire staff from applicants within the district helped ensure that a minimum of time and energy would be spent working with disgruntled staff members who sometimes present a challenge to new leadership in a school.

Del chose the planning staff of six, including the counselor and librarian, who then helped him pick teachers to fill the remaining 14 teaching slots. This may partially explain the unusually high morale, commitment, and mutual respect of the staff. One of the teachers said, "Del created the atmosphere. We also want to be here, and we assume we were chosen because we have something to offer. He's an excellent leader, but he has a good staff." When Del hired the teachers he was very clear about the methods that would be used and that all the teachers had to agree to work in the agreed-upon ways. When Del found one of the teachers using methods that did not fit the teaching and educational concepts basic to the new model, he reminded the teacher of the agreement made at the time of hiring and recommended methods the teacher had not used before. When she tried them out, she found they worked so well that she discarded all her earlier methods.

A teacher who had worked with four principals said, "When he greets me, I know he's made time for me. He sees things in a positive way. It's the strokes that he gives us that put things in perspective; it makes me realize how important positive reinforcement is for children. He brings both sides to the table, listens, presents alternatives, and then says, "Tell me what you decide." He encourages self-evaluation, then reinforces. You know where you stand. He keeps your value intact and yet provides constructive criticism; that's what I like best." Unable to quickly suggest any improvements the principal might make, the teacher's first response was, "I keep waiting for the other shoe to drop." When pressed for suggested improvements, the teacher finally said of Del, "If the error is one, it is that he's giving too much autonomy."

Another teacher said Del's number-one strength is that he is a mentor working with people. Her description encompasses high skills in both human relations and group leadership. "He's very positive; he's very personable; he's very approachable to kids and teachers. He's not one to give a pat answer. We have to bounce ideas back and forth. You have to think for yourself he's not going to say, 'Do this, this, and this.' His evaluation is detailed and he always gives an area to work on. He doesn't waste our time at staff meetings. We only have them when we need it. I appreciate that."

The counselor says of Del, "He's the best administrator I've had in my career. First of all, he works hard. He sets good examples. In goal setting, he gets people involved in decision making. He is enthusiastic and fair. He is decisive and he does his homework. When you do quality work he recognizes it. He takes evaluation seriously—it is objective and supportive." Asked about imperfections, the counselor said, "He gets in double binds." For example, the conflict between equity in education and sibling preference for current students is a problem because "the parents believe he should side with them."

Asked if there were hierarchical boundaries between certified and classified staff, one classified staff person responded, "There is no difference in treatment. Del [has] made it clear—we're a team, with no prejudice or elitism."

The custodian who followed Del to this school from another newer building said Del encouraged the custodian and the teachers to work out a solution when the teachers wanted part of the floor in each primary room carpeted for the younger children. Carpeting can create problems of both safety and maintenance, making extra work for custodians. They reached a compromise solution whereby smaller squares of loose carpet would be used by the children and maintained by the teachers. The floor would be clear each night to make sweeping easier. The bright cheerfulness of the hallways of the old school were the result of stripping the many layers of wax off the attractive but old, green-vinyl floor tiles, a task that had taken most of the preceding summer.

Del is "not just in his office. He's out on the playground. During my four-and-a-half-hour shift in the morning, about 18-22 percent of the time he's in his office. The rest of the time he's out roving." A parent said, "He's a very visible principal. He always has a smile on his face. He greets most everyone by name." This parent also directly addressed the openness of the school, saying, "I felt from the start that everyone's a part of the school—the students, the staff, parents, the faculty. Everybody's welcome here, not just the children. The staff is easy to approach. The parents appreciate being able to see the faculty and talk with them." Another parent said of Del, "He's someone you wouldn't want to disappoint," but not because he might get angry with you; indeed, she describes him as "unflappable; he steps in in his own calm way and calms us all down. He's not someone who loses his temper. He might get short but he's still courteous. I've had several bosses in my life and I've never had a boss as nice and supportive as he." Teachers agree, noting that Del often leaves positive notes for them, and that he writes notes on every single child's report card.

Del's school is an institution that anticipates change, resolves conflict, and recognizes imperfection. While the school has permeable boundaries and is seen as welcoming parent involvement, it still has a clear and explicit ideology.

Rather than giving answers, Del helps people ask themselves appropriate questions and facilitates their finding quality solutions. He exhibits high regard for teachers and their autonomy and recognizes them as critical educational authorities and professionals who can be trusted and entrusted with responsibility. Del shows a fearless and empathetic regard of students and models empathy from teacher to student in his own behavior. In other ways the students appreciate the way the curriculum emphasizes skills needed in the real world.

The coherence and wholeness of Del's school are impressive, especially in an old building with an obsolete library and a space shortage that means doubling up physical education classes in the cafeteria and using the library as a classroom for half of each day. Teachers are enthusiastic about their students, their curriculum, and, most of all, their principal.

A Soft Touch of Well-Being

Principal Dana's presence seems to permeate the physical appearance of her school. The meticulously groomed building, manicured lawn, and plantings in the front yard speak of a concern for an environment that not only houses but helps define and direct the educational processes taking place within its walls and on the playground. Although well over 30 years old, the building is more than well preserved. It actually seems to gleam with well-being.

This order continues inside the building, where the open main office invites entrance. On the right-hand wall of the entry way is a bulletin board with names and pictures of "Huskies of the Month" with their teachers. The hallways seem amazingly quiet for an elementary school.

Dana is obviously the source of this sense of "wellness" that permeates the school. An attractive, impeccably groomed, middle-aged woman, she combines a gentle manner with a fierce concern for "her" students, her staff, and her school. It does not take long to realize that, to Dana, the students' welfare takes precedence over any other consideration. When asked what makes her most proud, she answers—her face beaming with a wide grin—"Oh, the kids. They're just great kids." The fact that most of the students come from low-income homes, many from dysfunctional families, increases the significance of her unqualified endorsement of these students. Her assertion is reinforced by the current PTA president who says, "Dana believes there are no bad kids, just bad behaviors."

The culture of the school reflects this positive attitude. Warmth and encouragement are keys to the major themes that determine the philosophy behind Dana's administration: nurturance, involvement, flexibility, student-centeredness, and staff cohesiveness.

Dana has been a principal for only six years—three in a junior high school and three here. However, she brings a diverse background to her role as administrator. Early teaching experiences in Watts (Los Angeles) were, in her words, "where I really learned how to teach." Her experiences teaching in schools with diverse ethnic and socioeconomic compositions, as well as suburban middle-class institutions, have undoubtedly helped to establish the flexibility she considers essential not only to her own position but for the staff as well. "I like diversity. I like different things. That is not frustrating to me. I love change—I've done a lot of changing since I've been here." These changes have been in the physical plant, establishment of a computer center for 1st graders, improved staff morale and involvement, and student welfare.

Since Dana's arrival, much of the interior of the school has been repainted (significantly, one of the exceptions is her own office, which will be done last), and she has begun carpeting classrooms as money allows. In determining which rooms to do first, she avoided competition among the staff by using the logic that the lower grades would be done first since those children spend more time on the floor. A covered play area has been built, and she persuaded the PTA to buy banners to provide needed color in the school's all-purpose room.

During her tenure, Dana has worked consistently to eliminate any evidence of staff divisiveness and to develop their roles as contributing members in the functioning of the school. Her strategies have been as basic as combining what were originally two staff rooms into one to bring all members of the faculty together. But she has also used other strategies to ensure that staff members work together toward a common goal. At present, 13 staff members (out of approximately 30) are being trained in cooperative learning. This includes peer coaching, working out problems together, and sharing ideas and frustrations. Students are frequently shifted from one teacher to another if it seems to suit the child's particular needs to promote a better learning environment—always with teacher consent. This level of staff cooperation is obviously important to Dana. When asked what strengths she brought to the school, she thought carefully before answering, "Maybe cooperation among the staff members—that they feel good about working together. Even as a teacher, I always thought the worst thing that happened to teachers was isolating them."

The success of her efforts in this direction is confirmed by staff members. The special education teacher noted that the special services people are not forgotten but are part of the total program. Other staff members mention that Dana is always seeking input, and the custodian noted, "You couldn't find a better person to work for. . . . If you have an idea, you can go to her and she'll listen." Consistently willing to support new concepts such as cooperative learning, she gives her staff time to meet to discuss, implement, and evaluate new and existing programs.

One of the tactics that Dana uses to ensure this communication and flexibility is to actively involve herself in the workings of the school. She frequently steps in to assist a teacher and often asks to take over a class so she can learn from the experience. "She's aware of how she can be helpful," says a 5th grade teacher, one of the "old-timers." A staff member who is completely sold on cooperative learning and teaches a combined class of 4th and 5th grade students explains further. "Dana not only could but does model teaching." Besides providing a role model for her staff, Dana sees herself as constantly learning from them. She freely acknowledges the role the special education specialist has played in helping her to learn more about the needs of special students. "She's much younger than I am . . . but she has been my mentor." Another staff member confirms this facet of Dana's administrative style. "Dana is a student. She recognizes no one has more to learn than the principal. We appreciate that."

Dana manages to walk the often fine line that separates administrator and teaching staff, and it is here that the key to her effective management style can be found. She relies on an indirect, subtle approach in implementing whatever programs and policies she sees as desirable. She describes her methods of effecting change: "Start with really small ideas with one or two people and get them to involve people so that you're not always doing it. I think the principalship is this sparking of other people." By seeding ideas in this way, Dana manages to incorporate her staff into the decision-making process. The focus of responsibility is therefore diffused, and even difficult choices become easier to accept. "Once you spark one or two, then they can spark other people and get them involved, and then you aren't the one that's always stimulating change." Another advantage of this approach is that it allows her staff to digest new ideas before decisions concerning them must be made, therefore providing more and better input. The final decision, however, always rests with Dana.

Her ability to treat her staff as colleagues, not just in decision making but in the running of the school, becomes obvious as she follows her daily routine. Rarely in her office for more than a few minutes, she spends her day walking the halls, checking on classes, offering assistance and advice to teachers and students who need it. On a day when a substitute teacher was in charge of a particularly difficult 5th grade class, Dana was in and out of the room at least six times, not only to check up on the class but to help and offer suggestions. Whenever Dana enters a classroom, the teacher's face always lights up in a welcoming smile.

During lunchtime, Dana discards her high heels for jogging shoes and spends her time on the playground making sure recess is progressing smoothly. This gives her an opportunity to speak with the aides who monitor recess and, more important to Dana, provides her with an opportunity to interact with the students. In fact, she frequently joins in a game of foursquare, a favorite of hers.

The success of Dana's relatively short career seems most of all to be due to the nurturing that characterizes all aspects of her interactions with her school staff and student body. The students see her as "nice . . . doesn't ever yell." "Her office isn't scary." The extent of the affection she inspires in the children is evident in the spontaneous hugs they give her. She acknowledges, "Oh, yes. There are lots of hugs." One 5th grade boy came up to her and said, "You look pretty today." Rather than intimidate students, she encourages each of them and accepts them for who they are.

There are, of course, some discipline problems. When a group of boys is sent to the office by a substitute for acting up, Dana's approach is to say, "I'm disappointed you were sent to the office." (Significantly, she does not tell the students she is disappointed in them as people.) "What are you going to do now?" "It's your problem, not mine." "I want you to be cooperative. What are you going to do?" Receiving a commitment from them that they will follow the class rules, she sends them back to class. At no time has she raised her voice, but her determination to have them behave is obvious. When I asked if this approach to discipline works, she answers, "Sometimes." Later on in the day, she shifts one of the boys to another class to avoid further problems.

Whenever dealing with students whose personal problems seem to manifest themselves in negative behavior, Dana makes sure to sit so she can establish a more equal physical rapport with them. She leans forward and says things such as, "I'll help you work out a problem," or "I want you to do well. Can we try a little bit harder?"

This nurturing attitude extends to the staff. Her style is always nonconfrontational, although she is definite about her goals and tenacious in seeing them through. When she first came to this school she had problems dealing with a staff member who responded negatively to any suggestions for change. Describing this kind of adherence to set patterns, she said,

"It's great—that is always a great thing, but sometimes it gets in the way."
She eventually felt she had to secure an involuntary transfer for this teacher
and, even though she is not completely happy with her course of action, she
takes full responsibility for it.

Although Dana seems to have raised morale and established a well-
ordered, efficient school, she still acknowledges some problems. Parental
involvement in running the school remains low, with only a small cadre of
interested parents consistently active in the PTA. Next year this school
will pilot a program to integrate special students into the regular classrooms. This will involve some staff transfers, and she is concerned about
working this out so that all interests, the school's as well as the staff's,
may be served. "It makes me nervous because I don't know how people
are going to take this." When asked how she will handle telling the staff
about the program and its implementation, she concludes, "I'm going to
lay it all out—all the components of the program—in a positive way for
the school and for the kids."Once again, her priorities surface.

Despite her reservations, it seems likely that both the process of
finding a solution and the solution itself will be achieved through cooperative efforts of both the staff and the administration. But the ultimate
decisions will be made by Dana. Gentle in approach, she nevertheless
knows what she wants done and works unceasingly to achieve her desired
goals.

It is Friday afternoon, 15 minutes before the students are dismissed
for the day. Dana is reading to a 3rd grade class, which she does two or
three times a week so she can model for the teacher and, she hopes, spark
the students' interest in reading. Her sitting and reading in a soft, well-
modulated voice to a class of amazingly attentive 3rd graders on a Friday
afternoon illustrates as much as anything can Dana's concern for teachers
and students and her eagerness to be personally involved in the education
process.

Our portraits of these seven principals illustrate a variety of styles of
instructional leadership. It is interesting to see similarities as well as many
differences among the principals. In the summary that follows, we have
grouped their various behaviors into the four strategic areas of interaction:
resource provider, instructional resource, communicator, and visible presence (see Figure 4.1, pp. 86-87).

* * *

As noted in the summary, in performing their role as *resource provider*,
the principals use a variety of techniques: a lottery, special training of
department heads, released time for planning and observation of each other,

using teachers as peer coaches, and using a custodian to teach children, and using their own time to take over teachers' classes so that teachers have a chance to develop their talents. They clearly are investors in people.

In performing their *instructional resource* role, they model learning, share data and research findings with the staff, demonstrate good teaching by taking over classrooms, impress their teachers with their knowledge of the latest innovations in education, and inspire their teachers to use a variety of different instructional strategies. They spend much time in classrooms.

As *communicators*, they demonstrate expectations through modeling, use school-site councils, repeatedly talk about children and their developmental needs, model the importance of evaluation through self-evaluation, communicate the value of reading by reading to kids, and let the staff know that everyone can grow professionally. They display a high level of communication skill at one-on-one and small-group levels, and in articulating to everyone a vision of what the school is all about.

Creating a *visible presence* is not easy in schools. The conductor of an orchestra can easily be seen by all when conducting the efforts of others; school principals must work in less obvious ways. Nonetheless, these seven principals are perceived by their staff and students as effective conductors. They seem to be everywhere at once—always present. They articulate a vision about children and are perceived as fulfilling that commitment in the hallways, in their offices, in classrooms, before and after school, and at school events. Most important, however, their philosophy about education and children is clear. They are seen as articulate spokespersons for children.

Clearly, these seven principals find the time to be instructional leaders. They have placed a priority on providing resources, serving as instructional resources, communicating in a variety of ways to staff and students, and being a visible presence throughout their schools. This blend of technical and human skills enables them to orchestrate the effective functioning of their schools. Each clearly has a style, techniques that fit that style, and processes to take the actions necessary to achieve the vision they have for their schools. Each communicates a vision clearly and forcefully, no matter what the style. They have all found a formula for empowering their schools: vision, communication, positioning, and self-awareness.

Figure 4.1

Summary of Portraits Using Areas of Strategic Interactions between Principals and Teachers

	RESOURCE PROVIDER	INSTRUCTIONAL RESOURCE	COMMUNICATOR	VISIBLE PRESENCE
		Examples of Secondary Principals' Instructional Leader Behavior		
A L	• Uses lottery, observations • Regularly distributes educational articles to update staff • Departmental meetings used to develop curriculum • Seen as an aggressive fundraiser	• Models learning • Teachers sought him for feedback as they prepared for a presentation for a board meeting	• Communicates "I care" by being a good listener • Articulate spokesperson for not labeling kids	• Always seen in rooms, hallways, school events: "ever-present" • Accessible—always seen as having time for everyone • Everybody seems to know what he stands for
J A N	• Invests in the improvement of department heads through special training (e.g., CS) • Taps businesses and political leaders for school support • Uses staff talent in budget development through Faculty Senate	• Pushes teachers to expand into new ways of teaching for improving instruction • Shares data and helps staff interpret meaning of data for their school	• Lets staff know that everyone can grow professionally • Regularly gives staff members feedback concerning their performance • Regularly gives department heads feedback • Shares decision making through use of Senate	• Hall walker • Strategically selected her office in order to be visible • Master consensus builder • Always seems to be where the action is taking place
B O B	• Provides released time for staff to learn to work as teams • Staff ideas are used as a resource • Much teacher-to-teacher observation and peer coaching	• Spends tons of time observing teachers in classrooms • Inspires teachers with his knowledge of curriculum • Provides data concerning the school's performance to both teachers and staff	• Staff members know they must keep their feet to the fire • Accountability is prized and expected • Inspires others with understanding of how students learn	• Bob's businesslike tone is ever-present in the school • He seems to be everywhere • Parent coffee-hours are used to discuss school matters

Examples of Elementary Principals' Instructional Leader Behavior

S **A** **L** **L** **Y**	• common planning period to help teachers grow • Astute allocator of budget; gets a bang out of every dollar	• ing by taking over classrooms • Inspires teachers with her knowledge of innovations	• provement council to spread ideas • Communicates the importance of students and parents through involvement	• No matter what is going on, she always seems accessible
B **O** **N** **N** **I** **E**	• Pushes others' ideas to inspire others • Seeks out retraining needs of staff and provides retraining opportunities • Uses all staff members to teach children, including the custodian	• Uses classroom visits to stimulate teachers to use different instructional methods • Perceived as always getting people to talk about curriculum and instruction	• Leads teacher support • Communicates expectations through modeling • Uses themes and symbols to get across ideas	• She is seen as a "hall stalker" • Visible before school • Visible at social functions • What she stands for permeates the consciousness of both staff and students
D **E** **L**	• Carefully selected staff for the school when it opened • Uses self as a model for others • Uses four other principals to help him develop the new school	• Keeps staff informed about latest research findings	• Holds staff to commitments made when selected • Emphasizes developmental needs of kids • Models problem solving • Models self-evaluation by asking for feedback from staff • Often overheard giving positive feedback	• Greets busses every day • Always in classrooms
D **A** **N** **A**	• Spruced up the workplace by getting the school painted • Staff-to-staff development by helping each other • Uses her own time to take over classes to give teachers a break for their own development	• Models flexible and diverse teaching methods • At ease in discussing curriculum both formally and informally	• Communicates the value of staff opinions by seeking their input regularly on all major issues • Vision: Kids misbehave, but there are no bad kids • Communicates the value of reading by reading to the students	• Nurturing tone pervades the school • Always seen around the school • Forcefully puts forth the philosophy that all kids can learn

5

The Clinical Supervision Model and Principal Evaluation

Clinical supervision is "supervision up close" (Goldhammer 1969), requiring the supervisor to visit the school to observe the principal in action, to discuss relevant issues and provide feedback, and to develop a plan for the principal's evaluation. We have used the model described in this chapter for the past nine years and believe it is manageable, motivates the principal, and is worthwhile for the supervisor. It demands a substantial time commitment from both the supervisor and the principal. However, if the school district's priority is to support the principal as instructional leader, the clinical supervision model is a direct way to make it happen (Smith and Andrews 1987).

The clinical supervision model follows Bolton's cyclical evaluation design (1980) with three major sets of activities throughout the school year. These sets of activities, called "phases," guide the evaluation process:

Phase I: Designing the evaluation plan

Phase II: Collecting data and observing performance

Phase III: Analyzing the data and evaluating strengths
and weaknesses of performance

The "clinical" nature of this supervisory model demands frequent communication between the supervisor and the principal. It works best when the relationship is collaborative and when ongoing learning and professional growth are expected outcomes for both the principal and the supervisor. Face-to-face communication initiates the cycle with a Phase I conference.

Phase I: Designing the Plan

Three components of the design include (1) consideration of the school year and its unique situations, (2) performance goals for the year, with a plan of action, and (3) agreement on data collection and measurement. Each component is important to the design phase because clinical supervision depends on clear expectations from the outset.

Consideration of the School Year

The consideration of the school year and its unique situations is basic to formulating reasonable and appropriate goals for the principal. This activity leads the supervisor to examine collaboratively with the principal six variables that will affect her performance as instructional leader: (1) the environment of the school, (2) district goals and priorities, (3) school goals, (4) staff needs and interests, (5) student achievement and needs, and (6) suggested goals from the previous year's evaluation. At the Phase I conference in August, the supervisor and principal discuss each of these six variables from their perspectives.

The School Environment. The environment of the school is the context in which the principal will lead the staff, students, and parents. What is happening in that environment for that particular year? Is the student enrollment growing or declining? Is new housing being developed? Is the zoning or student attendance pattern being altered? Will the demographic make-up of the student body be altered through different patterns of resident characteristics? What is the condition of the physical facility? Are there long-term capital project needs to be planned, implemented, completed? Will the fields and recreational areas require modification? Have community members identified concerns that will affect the school? Certainly the environment of the school will present problems and opportunities for the principal. Identifying these possibilities enhances the principal's ability to allocate appropriate human and financial resources to meet the needs or to grasp special opportunities. This is also an opportunity for the supervisor to pledge support to the school through allocating district level resources, if needed.

District Goals and Priorities. District goals and priorities, established at least biennially, give direction to the principal's goal-setting process. What major curriculum areas has the district identified for special emphasis? How is research on instructional methods being used to provide inservice training for the staff? Are there budgetary constraints and reduction targets for the district? Has the board established new policies that require special action at the school level? What management team priorities have been established? Are student achievement outcomes a focus of district concern? Has district reorganization created a need to realign communication patterns between the principal and the central office staff? When the supervisor helps the principal consider district goals and priorities at Phase I, it makes possible the necessary networking and communication with the district, yet emphasizes the uniqueness and autonomy of that particular school. When clear goals are established for the district and school, the common direction and purposes allow the school to vary its means of working toward them.

School Goals. School goals affect the principal's performance goals. The principal's leadership in connecting performance goals to those of the school provides a model for the school staff. What goals have been established by the school's staff, students, and parents? What personal activities would support, extend, and enhance the achievement of school goals? What inservice training and research information would give impetus to staff efforts? What connections with the community might strengthen the impact of the school? Consideration of the school as a reflection of the principal's leadership will benefit goal-setting by assigning priorities on allocation of time and other resources for the year.

Staff Needs and Interests. Staff needs and interests may certainly affect the principal's goals. How can the principal provide new opportunities for experienced staff members to extend their skills and expertise? Which staff members might require intensive direct supervision leading to performance remediation? Are new teachers to be provided guidance and support in their critical beginning years? Will new teaching teams need some special attention? Have any teachers been reassigned to a new level or subject that requires them to engage in training or preparation? What inservice needs have been identified by the staff in the previous year? The principal should consider these and other staff needs and interests in order to provide the appropriate resources to assist staff members with their continuing professional growth and development.

Student Achievement and Needs. Student achievement and needs must always be a major consideration in the Phase I conference. After all, the whole mission of the school is to help students learn. In considering this variable, the principal and supervisor may review test data, new curriculums, parent concerns, staff concerns about student problems, and student performance associated with various factors. They may ask a variety of questions, such as, How are the students achieving in academic areas in this school? What about student attitudes and self-esteem? Are students experiencing stress, as indicated by illness, drug abuse, absenteeism, drop-out rate? Is career information readily available? Do post-graduate follow-up surveys indicate areas of need? A focus on the school's mission is critical to the principal's and staff's effectiveness. It can guide the development of the principal's goals and provide, in turn, a model for individual teacher goals.

Suggested Goals from the Previous Year's Evaluation. Finally, the principal and supervisor review suggested goals from the previous year's evaluation, which were developed when assessing the principal's performance. The principal will continue to strengthen skills and expand expertise as one year builds upon another. What conferences, workshops, courses, or other training opportunities would benefit the principal? What performance criteria will be a focus this year? Are district leadership opportunities available to expand the principal's perspective or to reinforce a special interest? How can the supervisor help the principal attain new skills and information? This variable presents many positive avenues for genuine collaboration and opens the door to the supervisor and the principal working together as a management team.

Performance Goals and Action Plan

Having considered the school environment, district and school goals, staff needs, student achievement, and suggested performance goals from the previous year, the principal and supervisor identify priorities for the coming year. It is important to focus on a manageable number of goals, usually from three to five. Once these areas are identified, the next steps include (1) developing behavioral statements of goals, (2) stating measurable outcomes, (3) developing appropriate strategies, (4) identifying time lines, (5) scheduling school visits and determining how data will be collected to measure achievement of goals, and (6) relating the goals to performance criteria.

Goals that are formulated in behavioral terms use action verbs. They are easy to break out, through task analysis, to specific strategies and action plans. The principal and supervisor discuss the goal statements in terms of behavioral or directional changes that the principal intends to make. For example, if it is a priority to help a teacher remediate deficient skills, the goal statement might be: "Provide an intense, structured evaluation plan that will result in remediating deficient skills in classroom management." Or, if the target is to strengthen the staff's participation in decision making, a goal statement might read: "Establish a staff advisory council with membership from each department." If the priority is for the principal to develop improved time-management techniques, the statement might be: "Design a month-by-month plan for managing time allocated to instructional leadership tasks."

Identifying measurable outcomes for goal statements is important. Taking the three goal statements from the previous paragraph, the outcomes could be stated as follows:

1. Provide an intense, structured evaluation plan that will result in remediating deficient skills in classroom management. The outcome of this goal will be the demonstrated improvement of the teacher's classroom management skills or the initiation of a probationary period.

2. Establish a staff advisory council with membership from each department. The outcome of this goal will be a functioning, decision-making body with clear lines of communication, guidelines for making decisions or giving recommendations, and written operating procedures.

3. Design a month-by-month plan for managing time allocated to instructional leadership tasks. The outcome will be a written plan that blocks out specific periods of time to be given to activities associated with being an instructional resource, resource provider, communicator, and visible presence in the school.

When the goals have been stated in behavioral terms with identified outcomes, the principal identifies appropriate strategies that will lead to the accomplishment of the goals. Following this activity, the principal identifies time lines for specific tasks and activities and schedules tentative dates for school visits by the supervisor. The supervisor and principal also agree on other means of collecting data to measure goal achievement. What information will the principal collect? A variety of sources may be considered, from observations or videotaped episodes to "artifacts" such as time records, reports, or surveys. In a collaborative clinical supervision model, the principal and supervisor are both responsible for gathering data, analyzing meaning, and assessing achievement. A useful format for recording the goals, strategies, time lines, and data to be collected is presented at the end of this section (Artifact 5.4).

Finally, goals should be related to the criteria that will be used to evaluate the principal's performance at the end of the year. Often, goals will "fit" more than one criterion. It is not so important to accurately categorize the goal under a criterion in the job description as it is to demonstrate that the goal reflects an aspect of the principal's performance that will be focused on that year. It also helps to highlight certain criteria in a given year, making the whole effort more manageable and attainable. In Washington State, law specifies eight general criteria for administrators' evaluation, for which each school district is charged with developing specific criteria. Relating the individual principal's goals to the evaluative criteria at the beginning of the year makes an easier task at year end when the annual evaluation is written.

Artifacts 5.1, 5.2, and 5.3 are from one school district's policies and procedures. They are included as real-life examples of the concepts in this chapter. Artifact 5.1 contains the district criteria to be followed in evaluating the administrative staff. Artifact 5.2 depicts the board policy, which establishes administrator evaluation as a cyclical professional development process. Artifact 5.3 is a job description for the principal, which correlates with the major criteria for evaluating the principal's performance.

Artifacts 5.4 and 5.5 are two different examples of a principal's annual performance goals, with associated strategies, time lines, and data-collection activities specified. These two designs are the outcome of a Phase I conference between the principal and supervisor.

Phase II: Collecting Data and Observing Performance

Phase II of the evaluation process includes the collection of data by the principal and the supervisor. Data may be grouped under two general categories: artifacts and observations.

Artifacts are written working documents, such as minutes of meetings, staff goals, action plans, survey results, memos, time logs, work calendars, budget reports, inventories, and the like. Artifacts of the principal's work year can be excellent reminders of progress and accomplishment. During Phase I of the evaluation process, the principal has made a commitment to collect various kinds of information to assist the supervisor with the analysis component in Phase III. It is easy to collect artifacts generated throughout the year if a folder is created for each goal. As information is generated, the principal merely puts a copy of an artifact into the appropriate folder. On the supervisor's school visits, it is productive to discuss current activities related to the goals and to share artifacts. The value of designating the kinds of information that will be collected is obvious—from the outset, the principal knows what to collect, what outcomes to measure, and what uses can be made of data. This simplifies the evaluation process and avoids the last-of-the-year pressure associated with a performance evaluation that happens just because it is the time of year to produce it.

Observations by the supervisor are a second major method of collecting performance data. At the heart of the clinical supervision model is the ongoing dialogue between the supervisor and the principal. Collaboration and collegiality can be developed through this process, which features (1) regularly scheduled school visits, (2) provision for feedback, and (3) a clinical supervision observation sequence for the principal.

Regularly Scheduled School Visits

A yearly calendar for clinical supervision is established early in the school year. The principal and supervisor determine which instructional leadership process will receive attention, depending on the goals established in Phase I. Tentative times are set aside each month (or more frequently if needed) for the supervisor's visit to the school. A minimum of two full clinical supervision teacher observation cycles is scheduled, and the supervisor observes the principal performing this all-important function. Faculty or advisory meetings may be observed, followed by feedback to the principal on group processes or dynamics. Reviews of the budget are planned for key times during the year.

Facilities may be surveyed as the principal and supervisor discuss capital project needs for the school. The principal may be observed disciplining students or conferencing with parents. He might be shadowed during a typical day, or the supervisor might substitute for the principal while he participates in a staff development activity. In each of the observations mentioned, the supervisor benefits from knowing the principal's territory and from direct observation of performance. The principal benefits from knowing the supervisor's expectations, from the supervisor's role modeling, and from the support of the central office for the principal's role in the district. Figure 5.1 depicts this concept of supervisory observations of the principal throughout the school year.

Provision for Feedback

Central to this clinical supervision model is the frequent opportunity for providing feedback to the principal. Formal observation and informal visits provide unique instances for dialogue and discussion about specific skills and behaviors. Following each formal observation, the supervisor holds a conference with the teacher and follows that with a written summary. During each school visit, the principal and supervisor may discuss a number of topics that are important to each of them. Keeping a list of such topics in a "communications" file helps to make the conferences worthwhile and productive and ensures that the administrators will take care of most items that are not urgent. (Of course, urgent items should be dealt with as they come up.) Certainly the principal needs to be kept fully informed about issues if she is to participate in district-level and school decisions. Also, the regular conference/school-visit format is a comfortable way for the supervisor to individualize the supervisory process for each principal. Principals, like teachers and students, have differing developmental needs and respond differently to supervisory styles. Individuals behave differently in a one-to-one conference than they do in a group meeting. Questions or

Figure 5.1
Calendar of Supervisory Observations

Phases and Calendar

Phase I	Phase II	Phase III
DESIGN	DATA COLLECTION	ANALYSIS/EVALUATION

------- ☐ --------------- ☐ ------------------ ☐ --------- ☐ ---------------- ☐

August	September	May	June 1	June 15
• Goal-setting conference before school starts	• School-based data collection • Two clinical supervision cycles		• Teachers evaluate principal	• Evaluation conference with principal

concerns that may not be raised by a principal during a group meeting may emerge during the conference with the supervisor. The conference becomes a nonthreatening forum for pursuing questions or concerns—or for discussing innovative ideas or testing hypotheses.

As part of the cyclical evaluation plan, a midyear conference is held to review the principal's progress on goals and to adjust targets or time lines if needed. This also gives the supervisor an opportunity to arrange for any district support not anticipated when the goals were formulated. This midyear conference is a good time to review teacher evaluation procedures and to determine whether any probationary periods will be scheduled. If such is the case, the supervisor and principal can plan together, designing a contractually accurate procedure and planning for needed observations, remediation strategies, and desired outcomes.

An Observation Sequence for the Principal

Because improvement of instruction is the desired goal of the principal's supervisory activities, we describe this part of the Phase II series in detail. The supervisor, in cooperation with the principal and selected teachers, models the clinical supervision process that is based on the format of (1) pre-observation conference, (2) classroom observation, (3) lesson analysis and plan for the teacher conference, (4) post-observation conference, (5) conference analysis and plan for the principal conference, (6) debriefing conference, and (7) professional growth objective. Figure 5.2 shows the flow of the observation sequence.

Figure 5.2
Model for Principals

Pre-Observation Conference
Between Principal and Teacher
↓
Pre-Observation Conference
Between Supervisor and Principal
↓
Principal and Supervisor Both
Observe Teaching Episode
↙ ↘
Principal Does   Supervisor Does
Lesson Analysis   Lesson Analysis
↘ ↙
Principal Holds Debriefing
Conference with Teacher;
Supervisor Observes
↓
Supervisor Prepares Post-Conference
Debriefing Analysis
↓
Supervisor Holds Debriefing
Conference with Principal

Pre-Observation Conference. Before observing the classroom episode, the principal and supervisor discuss the teacher's lesson objective and expectations, the principal's major emphases with this teacher, and particulars about the lesson that will be observed. The teacher may participate in this pre-observation conference, but it should be clear that the supervisor is there to evaluate the principal's skills, not the teacher's performance. The teacher and principal, as a result of this pre-observation conference, should know what to expect from the supervisor during the clinical supervision sequence. Will the supervisor take notes? Interact with the students? Be introduced to the class? A comfort level and climate of trust can be established when all participants know what to expect.

Classroom Observation. The principal and supervisor both observe the teaching episode and record data in the manner that was discussed in the pre-observation conference. Whether the format is to record verbatim notes, to use an interaction analysis sheet, to track certain types of teacher behaviors, or to videotape, the supervisor follows the same procedure as the principal. When the teaching episode is complete, the principal and supervisor leave the classroom together.

Lesson Analysis and Conference Plan. The supervisor and principal analyze the lesson independently, identifying strengths of the teacher's instructional techniques (referring to supporting evidence) and possible areas for improvement (again referring to supporting evidence). They each prepare a conference plan that specifies objectives for the conference in both the cognitive and affective domains. For example, cognitive objectives for the conference would specify what content the principal wants the teacher to know, understand, apply, analyze, synthesize, or evaluate. Affective objectives would specify what feelings the principal intends the teacher to have as a result of the conference, such as elation, comfort, concern, or anxiety. Topics of discussion that relate directly to the principal's objectives for the teacher conference are identified. These topics are references to specific examples from the observer's notes. Sample questions are formulated to engage the teacher in the lesson analysis and discussion. The conference plan should take into account the teacher as a professional and should be designed to suit the supervisory style preferred by the principal when working with that particular teacher—directive, nondirective, or collaborative (Glickman 1981). Also, as noted in Chapter 2, how the principal chooses to work with an individual teacher should take into consideration the teacher's general quality (for example, "superstar," good, strong, weak, or novice).

Artifact 5.6 outlines a lesson analysis and post-observation format, which includes the content presented above. Such a comprehensive analysis might be used with a probationary or "weak" teacher.

The supervisor may discuss the lesson analysis and conference plan with the principal at this point. This particular activity can provide for instruction or practice and is especially helpful if the principal is inexperienced in clinical supervisory skills or wants to strengthen skills in lesson analysis or conference planning. If desired, the principal and supervisor may role-play the upcoming post-observation conference and devise specific questions that might involve the teacher in analyzing observed data. The supervisor may refer back to the pre-observation conference to clarify the principal's objectives in working with this teacher.

On the other hand, the supervisor may defer the discussion of the lesson analysis and conference plan until the entire clinical supervision sequence has been completed. This depends upon the goals established with the principal in Phase I, as well as the developmental level and desires of the principal.

Post-Observation Conference between Principal and Teacher. The principal holds a standard post-observation conference to discuss the lesson in terms of stated objectives, student outcomes, and teacher behaviors. During this conference, the supervisor records data, similar to the procedure used while the lesson was being observed. Principal talk and teacher talk is recorded and special notes are taken with regard to specific topics being used by the principal.

Depending on the situation, the supervisor may take part in some aspect of the post-observation conference. For example, near the close of the conference, the supervisor might ask the teacher to indicate which observations by the principal were most helpful, or to describe what aspects of the observation conference could be strengthened. This activity depends, of course, on the goals and procedures agreed upon by the principal and supervisor.

Conference Analysis and Plan. The supervisor reviews data from the principal-teacher conference and determines the strengths of the principal's conferencing techniques as well as areas for growth. Modeling the same process the principal followed, the supervisor formulates a conference plan to guide the dialogue with the principal. Important considerations include the following:

1. Did the principal achieve stated objectives for the post-observation conference?

2. How was the teacher involved in the analysis of the lesson? Was the conference collaborative, directive, or nondirective?

3. What were the outcomes of this conference—e.g., a "negotiated plan" for future lessons, an "assignment" to alter specific behaviors, or a suggestion for the teacher to share an idea with colleagues?

4. Was the tone of the conference positive? What specific examples illustrate this? What feelings were expressed through verbal and nonverbal communication?

5. What questions were posed by the principal—at what cognitive level (e.g., if the principal's objective was to engage the teacher in analysis, were the questions analytical in design)?

6. Was the conference conducted efficiently within the allocated time? Was the pacing adequate for the teacher to formulate thoughtful responses to analytical questions?

7. How were observational data shared with the teacher? Were summaries, charts, lists available for review and analysis?

8. Did the conference leave the teacher thinking about future applications of content or follow-up efforts?

9. Did the principal follow established principles of learning for adults (e.g., relate theory to practice, involve the adult in his or her own learning, give concrete and specific feedback, provide clear statements, elicit the adult's opinions, use time efficiently, suggest further steps or opportunity to expand skills)?

10. At closure, did the principal check the teacher's perceptions of the major points of discussion in the conference?

Debriefing Conference. The supervisor and principal discuss the post-observation conference, following the plan. The discussion centers on questions such as the above, with specific references to the supervisor's notes or the principal's recollections. Throughout the discussion, the supervisor models the same clinical supervision model that the principal has used with the teacher, relating examples to teaching-learning interactions between the principal and the teacher. Usually, a professional growth objective emerges from this type of analytical discussion, and a new focus for the next observation may be set.

Since the goal of the clinical supervision model is continuing growth in skills related to the improvement of instruction, the supervisor and principal identify growth objectives for themselves. Growth areas might relate to the analysis of instruction, the planning and organization of the conference, or conferencing skills that emphasize the role of the teacher as a professional colleague. If the principal needs or desires further skill development, workshops or courses could be identified as part of the in-service plan for the year. Artifact 5.7 is an example of a discussion guide for the supervisor's debriefing conference with the principal.

Phase III: Analyzing the Data and Evaluating Performance

Near the end of the school year, the supervisor and principal have a conference to discuss the principal's performance based upon the designed goals and the standard evaluation criteria.

To prepare for this conference, the principal completes a review of collected data. He may be asked to complete a self-assessment similar to the one being prepared by the supervisor. Perhaps the principal will ask members of the staff and parents to give their perceptions of aspects of her behavior. Surveys such as the "School Assessment Profile" developed by Andrews and his colleagues at the University of Washington (see Appendix A) can provide valuable information relevant to the principal's performance evaluation and give an overall profile of the school.

At the same time, the supervisor completes a review of data collected during the year. Conference summaries, records of telephone calls and conversations, memorandums, personal notes, and observed data all are useful reminders of the principal's major activities for the year.

To prepare for the conference, the principal and supervisor might complete a conference organizer like the one shown in Artifact 5.8. They complete the organizer independently and discuss the content at the conference.

During the evaluation conference, the principal and supervisor analyze all of the artifacts and recorded observations. They identify outstanding achievements and tentative goals for the coming year. As the principal and supervisor move through this performance review, it is natural for new goals to just "fall out" from the discussion. Nothing is contrived or left to chance; rather, the cyclical nature of the entire evaluation design and process reinforces the concept of continuing learning and professional growth.

Following the evaluation conference, the supervisor writes the annual performance evaluation summary, using the evaluation criteria as an outline and citing specific information from the conference. There are no sudden surprises in the written summary; rather, it serves as a motivator by giving relevant recognition for the principal's significant achievements. It is also a stimulus for continued efforts in targeted areas. This document is a model for evaluation that can be transferred by the principal to the evaluation of the teaching staff.

A Time for Everything

How can the supervisor find the time to provide clinical supervision for the principal? Clearly, it takes a serious commitment of effort and quality time to make the plan work. If improvement of instruction is the purpose of the supervision, however, this model focuses priority time directly on that goal.

The time line of suggested supervisory activities (Artifact 5.9) is intended to provide a realistic model for the supervisor. We have used this calendar for supervising as many as 16 principals in 2 high schools, 3 middle schools, and 11 elementary schools. To visit each of 16 schools for approximately one-half day per month, we blocked out 8 full days (or 64 hours) for school visits on the monthly work calendar. When we used this calendar, the most workable schedule called for making the school visits on two days each week. In that way, it was possible to work around district meetings, board of director activities, conferences with parents and colleagues, and preparation and planning. We also supervised 10 other district administrators and 10 separate district programs and curricular areas (e.g., staff development, instrumental music, mathematics, computer instruction, bilingual programs). In fact, being "out and around" in the schools facilitated work in a number of these supervisory areas at once—much as the principal juggles several tasks simultaneously while "cruising the building." We found that getting out of the central office and into the schools made our jobs more interesting for us. We were better prepared, too, for questions from the public or from other district administrators about the personnel and programs we supervised.

In a smaller district with one high school, one middle school, and three elementary schools, we were able to implement this calendar with proportional dedication of time for school visits. Instead of getting in the way of accomplishing the superintendent's myriad duties, the school visits seemed to enhance the ability to provide district-level leadership. By modeling instructional leadership in this way, we emphasized in word and deed what was expected of the principal. We reinforced the importance of the district's mission—helping students learn. We put priority time and effort toward improving instruction throughout the district, not only in the classroom but also in the hallways, on the buses, and in all the district offices. There is time for this clinical supervision model—if the supervisor and principal dedicate specific times on the work calendar to attend to the activities associated with it. The following artifacts show a variety of ways of scheduling for clinical supervision.

In Artifact 5.9, we highlight major supervisory tasks for each month. Topics of conferences and school visits are also indicated.

Artifact 5.10 shows a supervisor's actual schedule for visiting 13 schools throughout a school year. In that particular year, new curriculums had been implemented for writing and science. The supervisor's visits to writing and science classes emphasized these areas and provided support for change.

Artifact 5.11 depicts a supervisor's schedule for school visits in a smaller school district.

Artifact 5.12 is a memorandum that was sent by the supervisor to principals before the annual teacher evaluations. The memo was intended to provide guidance and limits for this important activity.

Artifact 5.13 provides an analysis of a superintendent's time, similar to the research from Chapters 1 and 2 on the principals' time. [1]

---

[1]The artifacts, beginning on p. 102, are from W.F. Smith, "Artifacts from Superintendent-Principal Supervisory Artifacts in the Bellevue and Mercer Island, Washington, School Districts.

Artifact 5.1
District Criteria for Administrator Evaluation

Responsibility

The administrative organizational plan for the district will determine the responsibility for each administrator's evaluation. Each administrator will be evaluated on the basis of his or her job description with regard to established performance criteria.

Performance Criteria

The following criteria in italics must be considered in the evaluation of all administrators as appropriate to their assignments. Performance indicators, listed under each criterion, are examples that describe a range of administrative roles. These indicators may be selected, altered, or supplemented to fit a particular administrative role, department, or school. Such action would be based on a discussion of performance indicators by the administrator and the evaluator during the Phase I conference.

1.0 DEMONSTRATES LEADERSHIP, ADMINISTRATION, AND MANAGEMENT SKILLS FOR ASSIGNED PROGRAMS OR SCHOOLS

  1.1 *Demonstrates effective leadership of the staff, students, parents, and/or patrons.*

    1.1.1 Communicates a vision of school or department effectiveness.

    1.1.2 Establishes procedures to permit the staff, students, and patrons to review and formulate recommendations for school/unit goals.

    1.1.3 Budgets time to achieve balance between administrative and supervisory duties.

    1.1.4 Establishes appropriate procedures for development of unit needs and personnel selection.

    1.1.5 Delineates responsibilities and authority, establishes lines of communication, schedules the staff efficiently, and supervises non-teaching personnel and student activities.

    1.1.6 Communicates effectively through written and verbal methods.

    1.1.7 Is a visible leader and maintains frequent contact with students and the staff.

    1.1.8 Fosters a climate that encourages innovation, and nurtures needed change.

    1.1.9 Implements board policies, state law, and contractual obligations in a consistent manner.

    1.1.10 Models good instruction in staff and parent meetings.

  1.2 *Demonstrates knowledge and ability to implement approved curriculum or program.*

    1.2.1 Assists and encourages staff members to adjust their individual programs to accommodate individual pupils' needs and abilities.

    1.2.2 Assists staff members in evaluating their methods and instructional materials.

1.2.3 Schedules the staff in a manner most efficient for the adopted programs.

1.2.4 Assists the staff to develop meaningful goals, objectives, and strategies.

1.2.5 Provides leadership in building/department implementation of programs, ensuring that necessary resources are available to deliver the program.

1.3 *Knows and applies principles of school finance.*

1.3.1 Plans for budget development by formulating budget requests, establishing a time line for delivering the budget to the next organizational level, conducting a systematic process to involve the staff and community in developing budget priorities, and developing a budget document that reflects the goals and objectives of the district and school/department.

1.3.2 Requires the staff to use materials and supplies efficiently and economically.

1.3.3 Maintains accurate personnel, pupil, and financial records, and provides information as needed.

1.3.4 Processes financial data, handles purchase forms and procedures accurately, and audits accounts regularly.

2.0 DEMONSTRATES THE ABILITY TO RECOGNIZE AND EVALUATE GOOD PROFESSIONAL PERFORMANCE OF THE STAFF

2.1 *Acquires knowledge about staff performance through direct observation, discussion, and data-collection methods.*

2.1.1 Understands and models good supervisory and instructional methods, involving staff members in their own evaluation plans.

2.1.2 Demonstrates a sound understanding of effective instructional techniques.

2.1.3 Identifies and recognizes each employee's contributions to the district.

2.2 *Demonstrates skill in evaluating the performance of assigned staff members.*

2.2.1 Recognizes capabilities of staff members and encourages their professional growth.

2.2.2 Appraises staff performance objectively and fairly.

2.2.3 Uses observations and conferences to help employees improve their performance.

2.2.4 Establishes procedures for determining staff needs, expertise, and assignments.

2.2.5 Designs remediation processes, where necessary, to enable staff members to correct deficiencies in their performance.

2.2.6 Produces written staff evaluations that describe the staff member's assignment, evaluate achievement of performance goals, assess performance on established criteria, and identify tentative goals for the following cycle.

3.0 DEMONSTRATES AN INTEREST IN AND COMMITMENT TO STUDENTS, EMPLOYEES, PATRONS, AND THE EDUCATIONAL PROGRAM

3.1 *Provides an environment of trust that is responsive to the collective needs of the students, staff, and patrons.*

    3.1.1 Demonstrates ability to adapt leadership style to fit the needs of the staff, students, and patrons.

    3.1.2 Helps staff members to attain a feeling of security and satisfaction in their work.

    3.1.3 Demonstrates sensitivity to the feelings of others, and responds accordingly.

    3.1.4 Reviews accuracy and considers possible effects of information that is provided to the public.

    3.1.5 Avoids interruptions during time set aside to meet with individuals.

3.2 *Promotes and nurtures a positive climate in the workplace.*

    3.2.1 Furthers cooperation and teamwork among staff members.

    3.2.2 Involves the staff, students, and parents in decision-making processes, as appropriate.

    3.2.3 Organizes small-group and total staff meetings that are effective in providing guidance.

    3.2.4 Practices preventive discipline by means of open communication with parents, the staff, and students, based on clearly stated expectations.

    3.2.5 Provides for reasonable disciplinary procedures that are conducive to learning and are fairly enforced.

    3.2.6 Works with parent-teacher and other organizations to improve the service that the school renders to students and the community.

    3.2.7 Provides for multidirectional communication with the staff, students, and community.

3.3 *Provides opportunities for the staff to experience professional growth and to strengthen human relations.*

    3.3.1 Encourages excellence in staff performance through constructive suggestions.

    3.3.2 Encourages the staff to be involved in staff development activities.

    3.3.3 Assists employees to establish meaningful goals, objectives, and strategies.

4.0 DEMONSTRATES A COMMITMENT TO PROFESSIONAL GROWTH, AND MAKES EFFORT TO IMPROVE PERFORMANCE

4.1 *Maintains an appropriate level of preparation and scholarship or advanced training.*

    4.1.1   Keeps current by reading professional or trade publications.

    4.1.2   Writes clear, concise reports and other publications.

    4.1.3   Conducts workshops and gives presentations.

    4.1.4   Initiates and designs goals and methods for self-improvement.

4.2 *Participates in professional organizations.*

    4.2.1   Participates at the local, state, and national levels in appropriate professional organizations.

    4.2.2   Works with others in the professional association to promote legislation to enhance the public schools.

4.3 *Participates in workshops, seminars, and graduate studies.*

    4.3.1   Participates in conferences, inservice sessions, workshops, and classes.

    4.3.2   Continues to study in his or her discipline or field.

Artifact 5.2
Policy for Administrative Evaluation

Purpose

The purpose of administrator evaluation is the improvement of performance, which also strengthens instruction, student learning, and the operation of the district.

Evaluation System

The evaluation system will contribute to the achievement of individual and district goals, consistent with the district's educational philosophy and state law. The system will be implemented in a fair, equitable, and consistent manner. Administrators will be evaluated by their supervisor.

All administrators will receive an annual written evaluation, consistent with state law and district policy. New employees will be evaluated within the first 90 days of their employment. The written evaluation will become a permanent part of the employee's personnel file.

Evaluation is considered to be a continual process. The model for administrator evaluation will follow the cyclical model as outlined.

Phase I: Planning for Evaluation

The administrator and evaluator will hold a conference to develop mutually agreed-upon performance goals, consistent with evaluative criteria and district goals. Suggested strategies will be identified, and methods for gathering evaluative data will be discussed. If others are to be involved in the evaluation process, they will be identified. Parent and teacher input will be used when applicable.

The plan may be revised during the year by written agreement of the administrator and the evaluator.

If agreement cannot be reached for Phase I, the administrator and evaluator will submit the matter to the evaluator's supervisor for resolution. If the evaluator is the superintendent, the assistant superintendent for instructional support will resolve the matter.

Phase II: Collecting Information

During the time period covered by the evaluation, the administrator and evaluator will collect information related to the progress of the administrator in implementing the plan. The administrator and supervisor may each gather data from a broad base of persons affected by the administrator's professional performance, and they will use the data in a manner consistent with the evaluation plan.

Phase III: Using Information

Periodically, the evaluator will confer with the administrator for the purpose of assisting the administrator to improve his or her professional performance. Such conferences will be confidential, with two being the minimum number—one at midyear and one prior to writing of the year-end performance evaluation. Evaluative data will be shared, and analysis and interpretation of the data will be discussed.

Files

Only three files will be kept for the collection of evaluation information. These will be kept by the administrator, the evaluator, and the personnel office. If the administrator offers data to the evaluator as input for the written evaluation report, copies will be provided in advance to the supervisor. All copies of data kept by the evaluator will be discussed with the administrator. Copies of all personnel reports will be given to the administrator being evaluated. When the administrator terminates her or his employment with the district or transfers to another position, the supervisor will destroy all of his or her evaluation files. Only the personnel file will be retained as a permanent record.

Performance Criteria

Administrative performance will be evaluated according to established criteria. Such criteria includes performance statements dealing with recognition of good professional performance, capabilities, and development; administration and management; finance; professional preparation and scholarship; effort toward improvement; interest in pupils, employees, patrons, and programs; leadership; and staff evaluation.

Artifact 5.3
Job Descriptions

Job Description—Principal

The principal as instructional leader provides administrative and managerial leadership for the staff, students, and patrons.

The principal is expected to:

1. Lead, administer, and manage the school. Consistently apply board policies and administrative regulations, laws, contracts, and budget/financial accountability applicable to staff, students, and parents. Assess student needs; implement and evaluate educational programs. Provide for public relations with the school community, and ensure communication and feedback.

2. Recommend employment and assignment for all staff members assigned to the school, following personnel guidelines. Supervise the staff, and evaluate individuals' performances based on criteria and standards. Make direct observations, and provide specific feedback to the staff to encourage continuing improvement in performance.
3. Demonstrate commitment to students, employees, patrons, and the educational program. Establish an environment of trust. Promote a positive climate throughout the school. Provide structures and processes for school-based decision making to permit the staff, students, and parents to participate as appropriate in developing and accomplishing school goals. Encourage staff development. Administer a cocurricular program for students based on their needs and interests.
4. Maintain administrative credentials. Continue professional preparation and advanced training. Hold membership in professional organizations; participate and teach in workshops and seminars when possible.
5. Serve as a member of the district management team. Communicate and cooperate with other administrative units to achieve district goals.

The principal reports to the superintendent and supervises the associate principal(s), principal interns, certified and classified staff members, and students assigned to that school. The principal serves on the Executive Council, the Schools Team, and the Instructional Program Advisory Committee.

Job Description—Associate Principal

The associate principal is a member of the school's leadership team, serving under the direction of the principal and assisting with the overall leadership, administration, and management of the school. Each associate principal's specific areas of responsibility are to be delegated, described, and clearly communicated by the principal. The principal and associate principal will lead the school in a collaborative style that emphasizes teamwork and models participatory decision making.

The associate principal is an instructional leader. In that role, she or he is expected to assist the principal in all five areas of responsibility:

1. Lead, administer, and manage the school.
2. Recommend employment and assignment for the staff; supervise and evaluate the performance of staff members.
3. Demonstrate commitment to students, employees, patrons, and the educational program.
4. Maintain valid administrative credentials, and continue professional preparation and training.
5. Serve as a member of the district management team.

The associate principal reports to the principal and supervises certificated and classified staff members and students assigned to that school. In the absence of the principal, authority and responsibility will be delegated to the associate principal. The associate principal serves on the Executive Council and the Schools Team.

Artifact 5.4
Annual Performance Goals for the Principal
1988–89 School Year

Goal 1: Provide an intense, structured evaluation plan for _____ to result in remediating deficient skills in classroom management. Outcome: demonstrated improvement of classroom-management skills or the initiation of a probation period. (This goal relates to Evaluation Criterion #8.)

Strategies	Time Line	Data to Collect
1.1 Establish goals at Sept. conference with _____	Oct. 1	Written goals and plan
1.2 Make four formal CS observations	Feb. 1	CS records
1.3 Assign peer to "coach"	Oct. 1	Assignment
1.4 Provide six half-day release times for _____ to observe	Feb. 1	Reports of observations
1.5 Provide funds for _____ to attend classroom-management class	Oct. 1	Use of funds

Goal 2: Establish a staff advisory council with membership from each department. Outcome: a functioning, decision-making body with clear lines of communication, guidelines for making decisions, and written operating procedures.

Strategies	Time Line	Data to Collect
2.1 Discuss model and expectations with the staff	Sept. 15	Minutes of meeting
2.2 Provide for election of representatives	Sept. 20	Roster of reps
2.3 Establish procedures	Oct. 10	Written procedures
2.4 Provide training in group-process skills for representatives	Oct. 31	Record of sessions: supervisor observation
2.5 Assess Advisory Council functioning effectiveness	May 15	Staff survey

Goal 3: Design a month-by-month plan for managing time allocated to instructional leadership tasks. Outcome: a written plan that blocks out specific periods of time to be given to activities associated with being an instructional resource, resource provider, communicator, and visible presence in the school. (This goal relates to Evaluation Criteria #2, #5).

Strategies	Time Line	Data to Collect
3.1 Determine major activities by month	Aug. 30	Written plan
3.2 Calendar blocks of time for specific activities	Sept. 15	Calendar
3.3 Keep record of time spent on activities; note discrepancies between "desired" and "actual"	May 15	Time log; self-assessment of activities

Artifact 5.5
Sample Goal and Strategies

GOAL: #1: BE HIGHLY VISIBLE AS INSTRUCTIONAL LEADERS

(Area of improvement, or growth, or focus for the year)

Strategies	Evaluation of Strategies	Supervisory Assistance
What specific steps, activities, actions, or learnings will you use to accomplish this goal?	What data or information will you collect, and how will you collect it to indicate that you have accomplished your goal?	What can the supervisor do to support your attainment of this goal?
1. Complete two full observations, conferences, written summaries per assigned staff member	1. Calendar indicating observations and conferences	Superintendent can observe us and provide feedback
2. Involve superintendent and receive feedback in at least two observations	2. Copies of written summaries and evaluations in staff members' files	
3. Provide specific written feedback following conferences and on year-end evaluations	3. Staff feedback midyear and at the end of the year	Superintendent and colleagues provide resources as requested for professional development
4. Observe all staff members for short periods of time (informally) each month	4. List of building-based professional development activities	
5. Note and acknowledge staff strengths orally and in writing	5. Summary of student-oriented involvement and activities	
*6. Facilitate regular, ongoing, building-based professional development	6. Feedback from team members	
7. Provide resources, literature, and instructional ideas to the staff in conferences, staff meetings, and when requested	7. Calendar indicating teaching experiences	
8. Maintain high visibility in halls, classrooms, lunchroom		
9. Maintain active involvement with students in leadership groups and activities.		

---

*Indicates potential school goals

Artifact 5.6
Lesson Analysis Worksheet

1.1 Based on your observation, what was/were the objective(s) of this lesson? (What did you see the teacher and students doing?)

1.2 How did the teacher state or imply the objective(s) for the students? (Give evidence from your notes.)

2.1 Reviewing your data, list three teacher behaviors that you believe were significant in promoting student learning. Cite specific examples from your notes to illustrate the behaviors, and explain how students were assisted to learn.

2.2 Select one of the three behaviors from 2.1 as a focus for the post-observation conference. Give your rationale for selecting this particular behavior.

   Behavior to reinforce:

   Rationale for selecting the behavior:

   What actual words might you use in the conference to share this information with the teacher?

3.1 List one to three teacher or student behaviors that you have questions about or that appeared to be least successful in promoting students' learning. These should be potential topics to enhance professional growth and self-evaluation for the teacher. Cite specific relevant examples from your notes, and state the reasons why you believe these behaviors hindered student learning.

3.2 Identify one behavior from those listed in 3.1 to provide a major growth objective for the post-observation conference. Give your rationale for choosing this behavior as a priority.

   Behavior to discuss:

   Rationale for selecting this behavior:

   What actual words might you use in the conference to share this information with the teacher?

Plan for Post-Observation Conference

4.1 Outline the major points you wish to address in this conference. This outline will provide you with a "lesson plan" and should identify critical learnings you have as objectives for the teacher.

   Introduction, focus of conference:

   Reinforcement objective(s):

   Growth objective(s):

   Provision for sharing information (data) with the teacher and eliciting his or her input in the discussion:

   Plan for "teaching" or facilitating the teacher's analysis of the growth objective content:

Reference to the teacher's performance goals or ongoing growth objectives:

Reference to the teacher's performance goals or ongoing growth objectives:

Follow-up plans:

Provision for closure and perception check: What is the teacher thinking about as she or he leaves the conference?

4.2 What are your objectives for this conference? Note the reinforcement objective, the growth objective, and the affective objectives:

Reinforcement objective(s): (indicate the level of cognition for the teacher)

Growth objective(s): (indicate the level of cognition for the teacher)

Affective objective(s): (indicate the affective need for the teacher)

5.2 In your own words, how might you open this conference? Think about the tone you want to set and the style you want to establish (directive, nondirective, or collaborative). Write the actual words you will use in the opening remarks:

5.3 Considering your objectives for this conference, think how you will involve the teacher in the discussion and analysis of this lesson.. For each objective you have identified, write two sample questions or open-ended statements that would promote dialogue. Be sure that your questions or statements are designed to fit the cognitive level and the affective tone you have indicated.

6.1 For your major growth objective, prepare a short "lesson plan" for promoting the teacher's learning. How might you assist the teacher with analysis and synthesis? (For example, you might draw a diagram on the markerboard, ask the teacher to share a task analysis and lesson plan with you, show a set of data rearranged from your notes, view a videotape of the lesson and stop at preplanned points, or use a participation chart, etc.)

6.2 How will you know that the teacher has "heard" the major objectives of this conference? List some actual words you might use to have the teacher summarize the conference.

Artifact 5.7
Conference Category Analysis Form

Principal _____

Teacher _____

Supervisor _____ Date _____

As the conference is conducted, the supervisor will take notes to give feedback to the principal and teacher regarding these categories.

1. *Climate:* How did the principal contribute to a positive climate?

2. *Objectives:* Did the principal share the objective(s) for the conference with the teacher? At what level was the objective achieved?

3. *Questioning:* Were the principal's questions designed to elicit input from the teacher at the cognitive level planned in the conference objective? Was the teacher actively involved?

4. *Commentary:* Did the principal offer specific evidence to illustrate ideas or to give positive reinforcement? Did the principal refer to the effect on the students?

5. *Praise:* Were strengths recognized? Did positive comments relate to specific results of the teacher's actions?

6. *Nonverbal:* Did gestures, expressions, posture, and other nonverbal behavior reflect the same message as the verbal message?

7. *Balance:* Was there a balance between the talking of the principal and the teacher?

8. *Response:* Did the principal attend to the affective needs of the teacher? At what affective level was the tone?

9. *Closure:* How did the principal ascertain the teacher's reception of the conference? Was the teacher given an opportunity to suggest ideas or follow-up strategies?

10. *Comments and Suggestions:*

(Adapted from Kindsvatter and Wilen 1981)

Artifact 5.8
Form for Evaluation Conference

M E M O R A N D U M

TO:

FROM:

SUBJECT: <u>YEAR-END EVALUATION CONFERENCE</u>

    Your year-end conference is scheduled for _____ at _____ in your office. I am looking forward to reviewing your year's accomplishments with you.

    In preparation for our conference, please review the questions below and make notes for your own use during our conference. I will be completing the same preparatory activity and will be prepared to discuss my observations and augment them with data you deem important.

1. This has been one unique year! Considering my *assignment* this year, these factors have been significant and should be noted in my written evaluation:

2. After reviewing the administrative data, I believe the following areas should be emphasized in my performance summary this year: (Please include your *goals* under the appropriate criteria.)

3. When considering my own performance, I would like to work on some professional development areas next year. These would be as follows: (Relate these to appropriate criteria.)

4. Here are some comments about your work with me as area superintendent:

PLEASE KEEP DOING	PLEASE CHANGE OR STOP DOING

Artifact 5.9
Supervisor's Time Line
August 1–June 30

August

Hold a retreat for principals and other administrators to focus attention on the annual goals of the district and to develop teamwork and colleagueship.

Conduct a Phase I conference with each principal to set annual performance goals and to design the plan for principals' evaluation.

Establish inservice topics and a schedule of events for principals, with their collaboration.

September

Discuss with each principal the needs of staff and students in the school for this year.

Visit each school, dropping in to visit classrooms.

Establish a yearly schedule for school visits, and identify topics for principal-supervisor discussion during these visits.

Participate in inservice activities that have been designed for principals.

October

Finalize principals' annual performance goals, strategies, and activities. Begin Phase II.

Observe meetings of staff and parents conducted by the principal. Provide feedback on the group process.

Review school staff placement and staff performance goals. Discuss any staff remediation activities planned by the principal.

Review school goals, and plan to attend some special events at the school during the year.

Review enrollment projections for each school with the principal.

Participate in inservice activities that have been designed for principals.

November

Complete one clinical supervision sequence (pre-observation conference, classroom observation, conference, post-observation conference, debriefing) with each principal and a teacher.

Review student achievement, discipline plans, and school climate factors with the principal.

Participate in inservice activities that have been designed for principals.

December

Visit classrooms and attend special school events.

Review any teacher probation plans by principals.

Participate in inservice activities that have been designed for principals.

January

Conduct a midyear evaluation conference with each principal to review progress on performance goals.

Review the principals' procedures to involve the staff, parents, and students in decision making.

Gather input from principals about district goals that are being emphasized at each school.

Participate in inservice activities that have been designed for principals.

February

Complete the second clinical supervision sequence with each principal and a teacher.

Involve principals in district budget development activities.

Review program evaluations and curriculum needs at each school.

Involve the principal in identifying facility needs and long-range planning for improvements at each school.

Participate in inservice activities that have been designed for principals.

March

Review the school budget with regard to allocations and expenditures; discuss the principal's priorities.

Observe the principal's skills in conflict resolution and group processing. Give feedback.

Gain the principals' input for district goals for the coming year.

Participate in inservice activities that have been designed for principals.

April

Review format for the principals' written staff evaluations; discuss criteria and standards.

Assist with making decisions regarding any staff probationary outcomes; provide legal advice for principals if non-renewal actions are planned.

Discuss the principal's insights into and desires for next year's staffing needs.

Consider data from program evaluations that have been conducted; discuss action plans with the principal.

Participate in inservice activities that have been designed for principals.

May

Review the principal's processes and plans for developing the school budget for the next year.

Publish a district report defining progress toward district goals, using input from administrators.

Review evaluative survey data from the staff and community related to aspects of the principal's performance. Use "School Profile" assessments, if available.

Conduct a Phase III year-end performance evaluation conference with each principal.

June

Review the principals' written evaluations of the staff.

Write the performance evaluation for each principal, using the information discussed at the Phase III conference.

Evaluate the principals' inservice activities. Elicit principals' ideas for inservice topics for the next year.

Artifact 5.10
Supervisor's Schedule for School Visits

School	Principal's Goal Setting (Tentative)	Informal Staff Contacts	Principal's Goals Finalized	Writing Classrm. Observ.	Clin. Obser. #1	Principal's Goals Review	Budget Review	Clinical Observ. #2	Eval. Cycle Review	Science Visit	Goals Review
C.H. Elem.	8-19	10-21	10-21	12-4	1-15	1-25	2-25 8:00	3-18 10:00	5-5 8:00	5-20 10-12	6-11 8-10
E.G. Elem.	8-6	10-9	11-16	11-16	2-10	1-21	3-11 8:00	3-11 8:00	4-16 8:00	5-13 8-10:00	6-16 8-10:00
E. Elem.	10-13	9-3	11-3	1-21	1-21	2-23	3-10 9:00	3-10 10-12:00	4-15 8:00	5-12 8:00	6-18 8-10:00
L.H. Elem.	8-26	10-16	10-28	12-17	2-3	2-3	3-19 9:30	3-19 10:30	4-22 8:00	5-19 11:15	6-17 8-10:00
Med. Elem.	8-19	9-23	11-5	1-14	2-11	1-20	3.9 9:30-11:30	3-18 9:30	4-21 8-10:00	5-20 2:00	6-16 8-10:00
Som. Elem.	8-26	12-4	10-29	1-8	1-8	2-4	3-3 2:00	3-25 8-10:00	5-6 8:00	5-27 8-10:00	6-10 8-10:00
Sun. Elem.	8-14	9-30	11-2	12-10	2-4	2-4	4-1 10-12:00	4-1 10-12:00	4-21 8:00	5-14 10-12:00	6-4 8-10:00
Sun. Elem.	9-2	9-24	10-16	11-12	1-27	1-27	3-4 11:00	3-31 ?a.m.	4-29 11:00	5-26 ?a.m.	6-23 8-10:00
Chin. M.S.	8-27	9-29	12-9	1-14	3-17	1-28	3-17 8:00	3-29 8:00	3-28 8:00	6-2 8-10:00	6-24 8-10:00
Ring. M.S.	8-13	9-24	10-15	11-20	1-27	2-27	2-24 8:00	3-23 8:00	4-23- 8:00	5-21 8-10:00	6-9 8-10:00
T.Y. M.S.	8-27	9-30	10-29	10-29	3-18	1-29	3-9 7:30-9:00	3-29 12-2:00	4-15 8-10:00	5-13 9:08-9:53	6-9 8-10:00
B.H.S.	8-17	9-21	10-19	12-14	3-5	1-28	+CS*1 3-5 8-12:00	3-25 ?a.m.	4-16 8-10:00	will call 5-5 8-10:00	6-2 8-10:00
N.H.S.	8-28	9-28	10-12	10-27	2-11	2-11	3-4 1:00	3-4 1-4:00	4-14 8:00	5-7 8:42-9:34	6-3 7:30-9:30

Artifact 5.11
Supervisor's Time Line

_____ School District
_____, Washington
December 31, _____

M E M O R A N D U M

TO: Principals
FROM: _____
RE: School Visits—Schedule for January–May, _____

I know how busy our schedules become from January on to the end of the school year, so I would like to schedule some important times for us to meet at your school to discuss topics related to supervision, administration, and evaluation.

PLEASE NOTE THE FOLLOWING DATES AND TIMES ON YOUR CALENDAR AND CONFIRM WITH KAREN RIGHT AWAY. Some adjustments are possible, of course, but I would appreciate it very much if you could accommodate the dates and times indicated.

DATE		TIME	PRINCIPAL	ACTIVITY
1/15	Th	8-3:00	Evans	Observation #2; special video conf.
1/21	W	9-12:00	Matson	Observation and conference
1/29	Th	8:30-12	Galletti	Observation and conference
2/4	W	9-12:00	Smith	Observation and conference
2/4	W	2:30-4	Smith	Advisory Council
2/11	W	9-12:00	Cameron	Observation and conference
2/18	W	9-12:00	Matson	Budget review; goals review
2/19	Th	8-12:00	Evans	IC Meeting; budget & goals review
3/3	T	12-4:00	Galletti	Budg. & goals rev.; Prin. cabinet Mtg.
3/4	W	9-12:00	Smith	Budget & goals review
3/4	W	1-3:00	Snyder	Observation and conference
3/5	Th	8-10:00	Matson	Colleague Team Meeting
3/12	Th	8-12:00	Cameron	CCC Mtg.; Budget & goals review
3/18	W	9-12:00	Bridgman	Observation and conference
3/18	W	1-3:00	Nilson	Observation and conference
4/8	W	9-12:00	Cameron	Teacher eval.; Year-end eval. conf.
4/15	W	9-12:00	Matson	Teacher eval.; Year-end eval. conf.
4/22	W	9-12:00	Evans	Teacher eval.; Year-end eval. conf.
4/29	W	9-12:00	Galletti	Teacher eval.; Year-end eval. conf.
5/13	W	9-12:00	Smith	Teacher eval.; Year-end eval. conf.

SPECIAL NOTES TO HELP YOU PREPARE FOR OUR VISITS

TOPIC	PREPARATION, MATERIALS
Observation, conference	You and I will observe a teacher's lesson (please select a teacher I have not observed with you before this time). Following the lesson, I will observe your conference with the teacher, then debrief with you. (Please refer to our previous conference memo before this observation.)
Advisory groups	I will want to watch you "involving others in the building decision-making process" and would appreciate sitting in with your Advisory Council, Principal's Cabinet, School Improvement Committee, colleague teams, or Communicating, Co-ordinating, and Channeling Program.
Budget review	I would like to review your process for involving the staff in making budget priorities. I would like to see how you monitor budget expenditures and plan for contingencies and/or carry-over funds.
Goals review	I would like to see some samples of year-end evaluations. I will also share my notes from reading your last year's staff evaluations.
Year-end evaluation conference	Please use the new Administrators' Evaluation Criteria (with agreed-upon indicators) to assess your own performance. Make notes of activities and accomplishments for this year. I will have completed the same exercise prior to our conference and will discuss my data with you. Following our conference, I will write the evaluation in a narrative form and send the copy for your signature.

Artifact 5.12

25 April 19 ___

MEMORANDUM

TO: S/W Area Administrators

FROM: _____

SUBJECT: End-of-year written performance summaries

We are entering that time period when all of us will be writing the end-of-the year performance summary to place in each staff member's personnel file. For the past three years I have read these summaries before they have gone into the personnel files, and I am aware of the extensive effort that most of us put into these written evaluations.

Because I feel so strongly that this activity, while difficult and time consuming, is so vitally important, I want to remind all of us about some important components of that written summary:

1. The comments should recognize the staff member's assignment for this school year and any unusual environmental circumstances that have been associated with the assignment.

2. Throughout the summary, direct reference by name should be made to the evaluation criteria in the contract. It is not necessary, of course, to speak to each of the eight criteria, but certainly I would expect you to devote attention to instructional skills and classroom management. This reference to specific criteria by name is a critical element of each staff member's evaluation.

3. There should be a "summative" evaluation statement about the teacher's annual performance goals. Were they achieved? How? To what degree? Were there parts that should be continued to next year? Were there areas of outstanding achievement? How does each goal relate to the evaluation criteria by name?

4. As a summary section, note tentative goal areas for the next year. These should emerge by the examination of the evaluation criteria, the teacher's assignment for next year (if known), and goals accomplished this year. This is a good place to state again the positive aspects of the evaluation.

For those of you who have a number of peer evaluators, I expect that you will identify the components above for those writing the evaluation summaries. If the peer evaluator does not speak to the criteria, does not give summative evaluation statements about the teacher's goals, or does not refer to tentative goals for next year, then you, as supervisor, need to add comments to the write-up, as described in the contract.

Finally, as a reminder to all of us, start early—schedule the writing tasks so all do not fall at once; make the end-of-year conference a two-way discussion so the written evaluation reflects the interaction at the conference. Thank you for the excellent and professional job!

Review of Staff Evaluations

Evaluator: _____   Date _____

INTRODUCTORY REMARKS:
(years in district, position, unique factors, highlights of this year, etc.)

GOALS ACCOMPLISHED/CARRIED OVER:
(specific evidence cited, results, strategies, goals related to criteria)

RATINGS, COMMENTS RELATED TO CRITERIA:
(specific evidence of behaviors, events, examples of performance this year)

SUGGESTED GOALS FOR NEXT YEAR:
(outgrowth of review of this year's goals, criteria)

SUMMARY COMMENTS, CLOSURE:
(general comments related to entire evaluation)

Artifact 5.13
Major Activities and Time-Usage Comparisons:
1985–86 and 1986–87
for _____ Superintendent

Hours are approximations based on my calendaring events by function. Activities are reported under five major categories.

A = 85–86 First 120 days   C = 86–87 First 113.5 days
B = 85–86 Next 90 days   D = 86–87 Next 90 days

	A	B	*	C	D	*
Actual hours	1,394	1,076	2,470	1,196	1,045	2,241
Average workday	11.6	12.0	11.8	10.5	11.6	11.1
Average hours spent per day, per function:						
Office management	3.9	5.2	4.5	4.5	3.2	3.9
District operations	3.6	3.7	3.7	2.4	2.8	2.6
Professional growth	2.5	1.7	2.1	2.0	3.4	2.7
Board business	1.4	1.2	1.3	1.4	2.0	1.7
Outside contacts	0.2	0.2	0.2	0.2	0.2	0.2

SUMMARY OF FUNCTIONS: TOTAL HOURS

	A	B	*	C	D	*
Office management	464.0	467.5	465.75	513.75	287.25	400.5
(write, think, prepare, telephone, read, dictate, keyboard, etc.)						
District Operations	435.0	328.0	381.5	273.5	248.5	261.0
Mtngs. w/indiv. admin.	135.5	100.0		81.0	53.0	
Cabinet meetings	70.0	26.0		37.0	15.5	
Finance/budget	43.0	54.0		15.25	51.0	

			223.75	266.1
Staff meetings	27.0	35.0	18.5	27.5
Student events	26.0	19.0	14.5	12.0
PTA	24.5	14.0	12.25	12.0
Theory E	21.0	5.0	0.0	0.0
Cap. Proj./Constr.	17.0	27.0	23.75	10.0
Staff conferences	14.0	20.0	4.25	4.5
Student meetings	14.0	3.0	.5	.5
Fiscal committee	12.0	10.0	15.0	8.5
Writing column	12.0	2.0	0.0	0.0
MIEA meetings	9.5	3.0	6.5	1.0
Indiv. parents	9.5	12.0	5.0	3.5
IPAC	—	—	10.5	11.0
Student discipline	—	—	29.5	38.5
Professional growth	297.5	150.0	227.75	304.5
Professional mtgs.	65.5	49.0	74.0	108.0
Admin. inservice	62.0	17.0	56.75	13.5
Class. observ.	58.0	9.0	34.5	3.0
Presentations	48.0	15.0	15.0	52.5
Eval. conf./admin.	36.0	26.0	32.25 †	47.5
Clin. supv. obs.	28.0	34.0	8.00 ††	31.0
Principal selection			22.25	49.0

CONTINUED

* = Annualized totals (average of A and B, except for "actual hours")

† This figure does not include workshops given for ———— school district, University of Washington Seminar, or graduate class taught for Western Washington University, which were done during vacation time, weekends, or evenings.

†† This figure includes only the goal-setting conferences; other hours are counted under "meetings within individual administrators" under "District Operations."

	A	B	*	C	D	*
Board business	169.0	108.0	138.5	163.0	186.0	174.5
Meetings, retreats	72.0	63.0		87.75†††	84.5	
Monday letter	24.0	19.0		25.0	19.0	
Mtg. w/president	24.0	19.0		17.75	9.0	
Policy review	23.0	—		2.5	—	
Legal discussion	6.0	—		—	—	
Legislation	2.0	—		23.5	42.0	
Mtg. w/members	17.0	4.0		4.5	1.5	
ESD board mtgs.	1.0	3.0		—	—	
District goals				—	30.00	
Outside contacts	28.5	22.5	25.5	18.0	18.5	18.25
City, community	21.0	14.0		10.5	12.0	
Patrons (indiv.)	7.5	5.5		6.0	6.5	
Foundation	—	3.0		1.5	—	

†††This figure includes preparation time as well as actual meeting time.

6

Making Good Principals Even Better

Clearly, our clinical supervision model provides a structure for close-up supervision and evaluation. Those principals who are not instructional leaders experience the modeling, teaching, and feedback that can help them develop the skills necessary to change. Principals who do not have the ability or desire to become instructional leaders may be counseled or evaluated out of the principalship. But the true value of this clinical supervision model is the motivation, support, and enablement it gives to good principals who are trying to improve and enhance their professional skills. Following are some examples of this kind of supervision.

Selected Examples

A middle school assistant principal had been supervising a certain physical education teacher for 15 years. At a feedback conference with the superintendent, the assistant principal's discussion centered on collaboration—getting the teacher involved in analysis of the lesson and taking responsibility for suggesting growth objectives. The assistant principal reported that, during the post-observation conference with the teacher, he gave positive reinforcement for the teacher's skilled organization of the activities. But the teacher remarked, "Oh, I didn't think it was so wonderful. You know, I've been teaching for 15 years, and I've never observed another physical education teacher doing what I do. I just don't know if I'm that effective . . . and I do get tired of doing the same things over and over." The assistant principal said that instead of arguing with the teacher, "the light went on." Further exploration of the teacher's remarks led the assistant principal to provide several opportunities for the teacher to visit other schools to examine new methods and approaches and to work toward varying his units of study and teaching methodology. The assistant principal, through a simple feedback session with his supervisor, strengthened his ability to be an instructional resource to capable teachers.

A skilled elementary principal wanted to vary her clinical supervisory activities by inviting a teacher to be a part of the clinical supervision sequence with the superintendent. The principal videotaped her post-observation conference with the teacher, then asked him to assist the superintendent in giving her feedback regarding her conferencing skills and instructional analysis. The teacher appreciated seeing that the principal was being supervised through the same clinical supervision model that she applied to supervising her staff—and that the principal, also, developed objectives for professional growth.

One high school principal volunteered to work with the elementary science program. Part of his job was to give classroom demonstrations to help teachers implement new science lab kits. The principal taught a 6th grade physics lesson, which was videotaped. After viewing the videotape, 15 teachers who were enrolled in a clinical supervision course developed lesson analyses and plans for a post-observation conference. The principal and his superintendent role-played the post-observation conference in front of the class. Then the teachers compared their own ideas with those presented in the role play. This high school principal was willing to take professional risks to model the clinical supervision activities and to strengthen his own understanding of instruction.

Sometimes principals work with the superintendent to provide special recognition for excellent, "low-profile" teachers. An elementary principal asked the superintendent to observe him in the classroom of a quiet, highly skilled 4th grade teacher as she presented a lesson on expository writing. Both the principal and superintendent participated in the writing exercise and in the post-observation conference that followed. She expressed appreciation for the principal's and superintendent's compliments, which were tied directly to anecdotal records they had made while observing the class. She went on to make contributions to the districtwide development of criteria for assessing students' writing.

Still another elementary principal collaborated with her superintendent to gain insights about questioning and interacting during the post-observation conference. She wanted to provide a stimulus for a skilled primary teacher to self-analyze a lesson. The superintendent structured the principal's feedback session to model a series of questions and data analysis activities that led the principal to formulate her own conclusions. Following the analytical part of the feedback session, the principal and superintendent labeled the cognitive levels of the superintendent's questions and activities. The principal then developed a plan that allowed her to transfer this type of questioning and data analysis to her own post-observation conferences with highly skilled teachers.

Sometimes the growth objective concerns the tone of the interaction between the principal and teacher. One middle school principal, skilled in technical aspects of lesson analysis, asked the superintendent to observe for positive reinforcement and acknowledgment of skills during the post-observation conference. The principal developed a performance goal to focus on collaboration and positive feedback to create an atmosphere of support and motivation for the teacher. This principal developed overall supervisory skills through focusing on ways to deliver "negative feedback" in objective and supportive ways that led to improvement of the teacher's skills.

A high school principal videotaped the superintendent conducting a post-observation conference with a social studies teacher. She used the videotape in an inservice program for her department heads, who analyzed the post-observation conference and practiced their own conferencing skills. This principal worked collaboratively, teaching her staff the skills of clinical supervision, so that the careful observation of teaching and the feedback to the teacher became a norm of the culture of that high school.

Another high school principal found it helpful to discuss with his superintendent the remediation plan for a teacher who had been placed on probation. That principal made numerous classroom observations each week and received technical support from other principals and his supervisor. Over the period of a year, the teacher developed skills in preparing lessons and in varying instructional methods that resulted in students' improved attitudes and learning. The superintendent provided direct support during the development and periodic review of the remediation plan. She also was able to marshal legal and technical support for the principal to ensure the successful implementation of the plan and to provide professional advice.

Even students can participate in clinical supervision. A middle school principal arranged for the superintendent to observe her clinical supervision process with her assistant principal. Following the usual classroom observation and post-observation conference conducted by the assistant, the principal and the superintendent gave feedback to the assistant, using a three-way interactive approach. A student videotaped this sequence and offered remarks concerning the accuracy of the instructional analysis.

Good principals can enhance others' understanding of the model by giving presentations to other principals and central office administrators. One elementary principal participated with his superintendent in reviewing the supervision-evaluation model with the principals' supervisors from a neighboring district. The superintendent's perspective was contrasted with the principal's views about the value of the model. They cited specific illustrations of principal-superintendent interaction that had helped the principal to learn and grow professionally.

Another elementary principal participated in the school board's evaluation of the superintendent. He and the superintendent videotaped two sets of clinical supervision conferences in which the principal-teacher post-observation conference was followed by the superintendent-principal feedback session. To make things interesting, the principal and the superintendent switched roles for the second set of conferences. Yes, as the board could see, everyone emerged with a growth objective—the teacher, the principal, and the superintendent. The board, which had asked the superintendent to "show" them the clinical supervision model, quickly assimilated the steps in a good feedback conference. The board president concluded the superintendent's evaluation conference by asking the superintendent to give a summary of the strengths and growth areas the board had identified in the performance review.

Summary

The clinical supervision model can be a dynamic force in helping principals improve their supervision and evaluation skills, as we've seen in the examples of principals at all levels working collaboratively with their superintendents.

This is a model that nurtures positive morale, professional support, and collaboration as the principal develops and extends the instructional leadership role. It is a model that works best when used on all levels of supervision—when the school board supports the superintendent's efforts and the superintendent devotes time and energy to supervise principals "up close."

References

Alfonso, R.J., and L. Goldsberry. (1982). "Colleagueship in Supervision." In *Supervision of Teaching,* edited by T.J. Sergiovanni. Alexandria, Va.: Association for Supervision and Curriculum Development.

American Association of School Administrators (AASA). (1983). *The Role of the Principal in Effective Schools: Problems and Solutions.* Sacramento: Educators News Service.

Andrews, R.L. (1985). "Instructional Leaders in the '80s." Summary of research presented at the National Elementary Principals' Association Conference, Denver.

Andrews, R.L. (1986). "We Assume That Principals Are to Be Held Accountable for Excellence and Equity in Achievement Outcomes." *The Principal News* 13, 6: 10-12.

Andrews, R. (1988). "Illinois Principal as Institutional Leader." Report to the Illinois Association of School Principals. Springfield, Ill.

Andrews, R.L., and J. Hallett. (1983a). "A Study of the Perception and Performance of the Role of Principal in Washington State." Seattle: University of Washington.

Andrews, R.L., and J. Hallett. (1983b). "The Role of the Principal in Washington State." Final report. Seattle: University of Washington.

Andrews, R.L., and R. Soder. (1987a). "Teacher and Supervisor Assessment of Principal Leadership and Academic Achievement." Paper presented at the Annual Meeting of the American Educational Research Association, Washington, D.C.

Andrews, R., and R. Soder. (March 1987b). "Principal Leadership and Student Achievement." *Educational Leadership* 44: 9-11.

Andrews, R.L, R. Soder, and D. Jacoby. (1986). "Principal Roles, Student Achievement, and the Other School Variables." Paper presented at the Annual Meeting of the American Educational Research Association, San Francisco.

Andrews, R.L., A.V. Houston, and R. Soder. (1985). "The Search for Excellence and Equity: Seattle's Effective Schools Project." *The Effective School Reports* 1: 6-7.

Austin, G.R. (October 1979). "Exemplary Schools and the Search for Effectiveness." *Educational Leadership* 37: 10-14.

Bamburg, J., and R. Andrews. (April 1988). "Implementing Change in Secondary Schools Using Effective Schools Research." Paper presented at the Annual Meeting of the American Educational Research Association, New Orleans.

Bennis, W. (August 1984). "The 4 Competencies of Leadership." *Training and Development Journal* 38, 8: 15-19.

Bennis, W., and B. Nanus. (1985). *Leaders: The Strategies for Taking Charge*. New York: Harper and Row.

Bents, H., and K.R. Howey. (1981). "Staff Development: Change in the Individual." In *Staff Development/Organization Development*, edited by B. Dillon-Peterson. Alexandria, Va.: Association for Supervision and Curriculum Development.

Blumberg, A., and W. Greenfield. (1980). *The Effective Principal: Perspectives on School Leadership*. Boston: Allyn and Bacon.

Bolton, D. (1973). *Selection and Evaluation of Teachers*. Berkeley, Calif.: McCutchan.

Bolton, D. (1980). *Evaluating Administrative Personnel in School Systems*. New York: Teachers College Press.

Bossert, S., D. Dwyer, B. Rowan, and G. Lee. (1981). *The Instructional Management Role of the Principal: A Preliminary Conceptualization*. San Francisco: Far West Regional Laboratory for Educational Research and Development.

Brookover, W.B., and L.W. Lezotte. (1977). "Changes in School Characteristics Coincident with Changes in Student Achievement." Occasional Paper No. 17. East Lansing, Mich.: University Institute for Research on Teaching.

Brookover, W.L., L. Beamer, H. Esthin, D. Hathaway, L. Lezotte, S. Miller, J. Passalacqua, and L. Tornetzky. (1982). *Creating Effective School*. Holmes Beach, Fla.: Learning Publications.

Cawelti, G. (1984). "Behavior Patterns of Effective Principals." *Phi Delta Kappan* 41: 3.

Dow, I.I., and R.Y. Whitehead. (September 1980). "Curriculum Implementation Study. Physical Education K-6: Personal Well-Being." Final report funded under contract with the Carlton Board of Education, University of Ottowa.

Dwyer, D. (1984). "The Search for Instructional Leadership Routines and Subtleties in the Principal's Role." *Educational Leadership* 41: 32-37.

Edmonds, R. (October 1979). "Effective Schools for the Urban Poor." *Educational Leadership*. 22: 22-23.

Edmonds, R. (February 1982). Speech on his effective-schools research presented at the Annual Conference of the Washington State Association of Supervision and Curriculum Development, Seattle, Washington.

Estler, S. (April 1985). "Clear Goals, Instructional Leadership, and Academic Achievement: Implementation and Findings." Paper presented at the American Educational Research Association Conference, Chicago.

Frederickson, J.R., and R.R. Edmonds. (1979). "Identification of Instructionally Effective and Ineffective Schools." Paper presented at the Annual Meeting of the American Educational Research Association, San Francisco.

Fullan, M. (1981). *The Meaning of Educational Change*. New York: Teachers College Press.

Gauthier, W.J., Jr. (October 1980). "Focusing for Effectiveness." *Choices* 4, 7: 16, 17.

Giammetteo, M.C., and D.W. Giammetteo. (1981). *Forces on Leadership*. Reston, Va.: National Association of Secondary School Principals.

Glasman, N.S. (1979). "Student Achievement and the School Principal." *Educational Evaluation and Policy Analysis* 3: 283-296.

Glatthorn, A.A. (1984). *Differentiated Supervision*. Alexandria, Va.: Association for Supervision and Curriculum Development.

Glickman, C.D. (1981). *Developmental Supervision*. Alexandria, Va.: Association for Supervision and Curriculum Development.

Goldhammer, R. (1969). *Clinical Supervision*. New York: Holt Rinehart and Winston.

Goodlad, J.I. (1984). *A Place Called School: Prospects for the Future*. New York: McGraw-Hill.

Gross, G., M. Bernstein, and J. Giacquinta. (1971). *Implementing Organizational Innovations: A Sociological Analysis of Planned Educational Change*. New York: Basic Books.

Hall, G., W. Rutherford, S. Hord, and L. Huling. (February 1984). "Effects of Three Principal Styles on School Improvement." *Educational Leadership* 41: 22-29.

Hallinger, P., and J. Murphey. (1985). "Assessing the Instructional Management Behavior of Principals." *Elementary School Journal* 85: 217-247.

Herzberg, F., B. Mauser, and B. Snyderman. (1959). *The Motivation to Work*. New York: Wiley.

Iannaccone, L., and R. Jamgochian. (May 1985). "High Performing Curriculum and Instructional Leadership in the Climate of Excellence." *NASSP Bulletin* 69: 28-35.

Joyce, B.R., R.H. Hersh, and M. McKibbin. (1983). *The Structure of School Improvement*. New York: Longman.

Joyce, B.R., and B. Showers. (1983). *Power in Staff Development Through Research on Training*. Alexandria, Va.: Association for Supervision and Curriculum Development.

Kahn, R.L., and R.A. Rosenthal. (1964). *Organizational Stress: Studies in Role Conflict and Ambiguity*. New York: Wiley.

Kindsvatter, R., and W. Wilen. (April 1981). "A Systematic Approach to Improving Conference Skills." *Educational Leadership*. 38: 525-529.

Knowles, M. (1978). *The Adult Learner: A Neglected Species*. Houston: Gulf.

Krajewski, R.J. (September 1978). "Secondary Principals Want to Be Instructional Leaders." *Phi Delta Kappan* 60: 65-69.

Lake Washington School District (LWSD). (1980). Building Administration Analysis, Lake Washington School District, Kirkland, Washington.

Leithwood, K., and D. Montgomery. (1982). "The Role of the Elementary Principal in Program Improvement." *Review of Educational Research* 52: 309-339.

Lezotte, L., and J. Passalacqua. (1978). "Individual School Buildings: Accounting for Differences in Measured Pupil Performance." *Urban Education* 13: 283-293.

Lipham, J.M. (1981). *Effective Principal, Effective School*. Reston, Va.: National Association of Secondary School Principals.

Little, J.W. (Fall 1982). "Norms of Collegiality and Experimentation: Workplace Conditions of School Success." *American Educational Research Journal* 19: 325-340.

Lord, R.G., J.S. Phillips, and M.C. Rush. (1980). "Effects of Sex and Personality on Perceptions of Emergent Leadership, Influence, and Social Power." *Journal of Applied Psychology* 65: 176-182.

Lovell, J.T., and K. Wiles. (1983). *Supervision for Better Schools*. Englewood Cliffs, N.J.: Prentice-Hall.

Manasse, L.A. (February 1984). "Principals as Leaders of High-Performing Systems." *Educational Leadership* 41: 24-46.

McCormack-Larkin, M. (1985). "Ingredients of a Successful School Effectiveness Project." *Phi Delta Kappan* 42: 38-43.

Nebecker, D.M., and T.R. Mitchell. (1974). "Leadership Behavior: An Expectancy Approach." *Organizational Behavior and Human Performance* 11: 355-367.

Osborn, R.N., and J.G. Hunt. (1975). "An Adaptive-Reactive Theory of Leadership: The Role of Macro Variables in Leadership Research." In *Leadership Frontiers*, edited by J.G. Hunt and L.L. Larson. Kent, Ohio: Kent State University Press.

Osborn, R.N., and J.G. Hunt. (1978). "A Multiple Influence Approach to Leadership for Managers." In *Leadership for Practitioners*, edited by J. Stinson and P. Hersey. Athens, Ohio: Center for Leadership Studies.

Persell, C., and P. Cookson. (1982). "The Effect of Principals in Action." In *The Effective Principal: A Research Summary*. Reston, Va.: National Association of Secondary School Principals.

Petrie, T.A., and B. Burton. (May 1980). "Levels of Leader Development." *Educational Leadership* 37: 628-631.

Pfeffer, J., and G.R. Salancik. (1975). "Determinants of Supervisory Behavior: A Role Set Analysis." *Human Relations* 28: 139-153.

Powell, A.G., E. Farrar, and D.K. Cohen. (1985). *The Shopping Mall High School: Winners and Losers in the Educational Marketplace.* Boston: Houghton Mifflin.

Purkey, S.C., and M.S. Smith. (December 1982). "Too Soon to Cheer? Synthesis of Research on Effective Schools." *Educational Leadership* 40: 64-69.

Reinhardt, D., R. Arends, M. Burns, W. Kutz, and S. Wyant. (July 1979). "A Study of the Principal's Role in Externally Funded Change Projects and the Implication of/for Inservice Training." Vol. 1. A technical report for the University of Oregon Teacher Corps Project.

Revised Code of Washington (State). (1980). Chapter 28, Section A. 67. Seattle, Wa.: Book Publishing Company.

Roe, W.H., and T.L. Drake. (1980). *The Principalship.* New York: Macmillan Publishing Co.

Rosenblum, S., and J. Jastrzab. (1975). "The Surveys of the International Association for the Evaluation of Educational Achievement (IEA): Implications of the IEA Surveys of Achievement." In *Educational Policy and International Assessment,* edited by A.C. Purvis and D.V. Levine. Berkeley, Ca.: McCutchan.

Rutherford, W. (1985). "School Principals as Effective Leaders." *Phi Delta Kappan* 67: 31-34.

Rutter, M., B. Maughan, P. Mortimore, J. Outson, and A. Smith. (1979). *Fifteen Thousand Hours: Secondary Schools and Their Effects on Children.* Cambridge, Mass.: Harvard University Press.

Sarason, S.B. (1971). *The Culture of the School and the Problem of Change.* Boston: Allyn and Bacon.

Sapone, C.O. (Winter 1985). "Curriculum: The Basis for Instructional Leadership, the Principal's Role." *Catalyst for Change* 14: 4-7.

Schmuck, R. (October 1985). "Leadership for Organizational Development." Paper presented at the Conference of the Washington Association of School Administrators, Bellevue.

Schon, D.A. (1983). *The Reflective Practitioner: How Principals Think in Action.* New York: Basic Books.

Sergiovanni, T.J., ed. (1975). *Professional Supervision for Professional Teachers.* Alexandria, Va.: Association for Supervision and Curriculum Development.

Sergiovanni, T.J. (1984). "Leadership and Excellence in Schooling." *Phi*

Delta Kappan 41: 4-13.

Smith, W.F. (1989). *School-Based Management: Metaphor for Motivation.* Olympia: Association of Washington School Principals.

Smith, W.F., and R.L. Andrews. (September 1987). "Clinical Supervision for Principals." *Educational Leadership* 45: 34-37.

Soder, R., and R.L. Andrews. (Summer 1985). "The Moral Imperatives of Compulsory Schooling." *Curriculum in Context* 6-8, 12.

Vail, P. (Autumn 1982). "The Purposing of High Performing Systems." *Organizational Dynamics* 11, 2: 23-39.

Weick, C.E. (1982). "Administering Education in Loosely Coupled Schools." *Phi Delta Kappan* 27: 673-676.

Wilson, K. (1982). "An Effective School Principal." *Educational Leadership* 39: 357-61.

Wing, D.J. (1987). "The Examination of Staff Perceptions of the Importance of Characteristics Associated with Strong Instructional Leadership at the Elementary, Middle, and High School Levels." Doctoral diss., University of Washington.

Wood, F.H., and S.R. Thompson. (February 1980). "Guidelines for Better Staff Development." *Educational Leadership* 37: 374-378.

Wynne, E.A. (1980). *Looking at Schools: Good, Bad, and Indifferent.* Lexington, Mass.: D.C. Heath.

Yukl, G.A. (1981). *Leadership in Organizations.* Englewood Cliffs, N.J.: Prentice-Hall.

Appendix

Observations of average and strong instructional leader principals suggest that they value the same things about their jobs, but strong instructional leaders are less distracted by routine tasks and maintain focus on curriculum and instruction. Thus, the amount of time principals spend on the various dimensions of their job is important.

On the pages that follow are displays of the time distribution of the average principal and the strong instructional leader principal, a Zero-Based Job Analysis Questionnaire, and a Time-Log Sheet. These documents can help principals gain a better understanding of the aspects of their job that they value most, how they can use their time effectively, and in which areas they need to restructure their time to focus more on instructional improvement matters.

Zero-Based Job Analysis Questionnaire

Included in this assessment instrument are 160 tasks identified by the National Association of Secondary School Principals as activities that principals perform on a day-to-day basis in order to do the job normally assigned to them by their school district.

The questionnaire is designed to help school administrators take a critical look at the job of the principal and determine who should perform these tasks.

Directions: Beginning on the next page is a list of tasks that represent many of the possible activities expected of school principals. Assume that this is a zero-based job description—that is, you can describe the job as it should be performed, not as someone else has defined it. Thus, you may assume all of these responsibilities or delegate some or all of them to others.

Use the following rating values in making your judgments, and mark A, B, or C in the column on the right labeled "Rating Values."

    A = an activity I would keep for myself.
    B = an activity I would delegate to a vice principal or other professional person on my staff.
    C = an activity the central office should take care of.

(The numbers in parentheses on the left are explained later in the instructions for scoring.)

Zero-Based Job Description   **Rating Values**

(1)   1. Provides inservice training for teachers to increase their _____ effectiveness.

(4)   2. Supervises job performance of custodial, secretarial, or _____ other support staff.

(1)   3. Plans, develops, and implements a process for student, _____ teacher, and parent involvement in determining curriculum goals and objectives.

(3)   4. Organizes community members to lobby for support for _____ programs in which he/she/community have a special interest.

(7)   5. Meets with various parties involved (teachers, parents, _____ students, and professional people) in accordance with legal requirements.

(3)   6. Communicates with the public concerning the nature and _____ rationale of various school programs.

(5)   7. Organizes a system for dealing with discipline problems. _____

(5)   8. Exercises leadership role in developing mechanisms for _____ integration of various cultural groups in the school.

(1)   9. Assigns teachers/professional staff to classes. _____

(7) 10. Establishes communication lines with other principals in _____ the district.

(3) 11. Works with booster clubs to raise money for various _____ school needs or activities.

(1) 12. Encourages and helps the faculty to develop innovative _____ teaching methods.

(6) 13. Monitors disciplinary actions involving students to ensure _____ due process is followed.

(4) 14. Reports to the district on nature and cleanliness of the _____ building and its maintenance.

(4) 15. Sets standards; communicates and monitors standards _____ for orderly maintenance of school facilities.

(5) 16. Develops standards, objectives, and procedures to maintain counseling services. _____

(6) 17. Selects and supervises safety patrols. _____

(4) 18. Monitors or oversees free-lunch program to ensure that _____ appropriate students receive lunches.

(6) 19. Coordinates with local police to ensure smooth function- ____
ing of school, both during school hours and after school
at extracurricular activities.

(3) 20. Seeks to know the parents and to interpret the school's ____
programs to them.

(5) 21. Organizes activities and provides space for school psy- ____
chologists, speech pathologists, and similar professionals.

(4) 22. Follows established district procedures for selection of ____
new maintenance staff members.

(4) 23. Arranges transportation of students to extracurricular ____
events.

(3) 24. Helps the community raise money for the United Fund ____
and other charitable or service organizations.

(3) 25. Provides training for staff members to enable them to ____
deal with parents and community.

(3) 26. Responds to requests for input or ideas on various com- ____
munity programs and activities not directly involving the
school.

(6) 27. Determines, communicates, and maintains standards for ____
participation in student activities.

(1) 28. Determines student interest in new courses and encour- ____
ages their development.

(5) 29. Elicits student participation in student government. ____

(3) 30. Participates in various community agencies and con- ____
cerns—not solely academic (Kiwanis, churches, Cham-
ber of Commerce, Lion's Club, senior citizens groups,
etc.).

(7) 31. Monitors the racial/sexual composition of student groups ____
and the compliance of the school with the provisions of
Title IX.

(5) 32. Coordinates programs with various agencies—employing ____
students in co-ops.

(4) 33. Ensures that approved budget monies are received. ____

(2) 34. Recruits applicants for staff positions. ____

(4) 35. Responds to requests for information, paperwork, annual ____
reports, etc., from district.

(5) 36. Strives to know and understand students and considers ___ requests.

(6) 37. Approves, oversees, and works with student fundraising ___ efforts/exercises.

(5) 38. Communicates with nurses, health officials, parents, ___ etc., so that students' special health problems (e.g., allergies, epilepsy) can be recognized.

(6) 39. Reviews the number and nature of student activities ___ or establishes a system to review and eliminate or add activities.

(1) 40. Organizes programs to evaluate students' competencies. ___

(6) 41. Selects and assigns staff to direct extracurricular ___ activities.

(4) 42. Monitors the expenditure of funds raised by booster ___ clubs, other community groups, or student activities.

(1) 43. Sets up strategies to implement activities, priorities, and ___ programs set at the district level.

(6) 44. Patrols parking lots. ___

(4) 45. Maintains accessibility to students, parents, teachers, ___ and other groups interested in school activities.

(4) 46. Provides teachers with uniform procedures for keeping ___ and reporting attendance.

(1) 47. Helps staff members set professional goals. ___

(5) 48. Solicits and coordinates parent volunteers and coopera- ___ tion in school committees, tutor pool, health services, etc., and other school activities.

(4) 49. Meets with and informs parents and health officials re- ___ garding various school problems, including nutrition and immunizations.

(1) 50. Implements and refines what is developed by central of- ___ fice in the area of curriculum.

(2) 51. Establishes orientation for new teachers/staff. ___

(7) 52. Seeks resource alternatives within and outside district if ___ original proposals are not accepted.

(2) 53. Provides feedback to teachers concerning their perfor- ___ mance.

(5) 54. Deals with conflicts that arise among teacher/student/ ___ parent/support-staff relationships.

(1) 55. Monitors the staff to determine the extent to which cur- ____
riculum goals and objectives are being met.

(7) 56. Writes grant proposals to seek money from district, ____
county, and federal sources.

(4) 57. Schedules work hours of support staff.   ____

(5) 58. Sets up procedures to deal with ill or injured students. ____

(6) 59. Encourages and secures parent involvement in student ____
activities as participants and chaperones.

(3) 60. Elicits community sponsorship of school programs. ____

(8) 61. Maintains current knowledge of union-management con- ____
tracts in order to develop personnel policies consistent
with their provisions.

(6) 62. Supervises the lunchroom. ____

(4) 63. Coordinates with district to procure equipment to render ____
services for transportation needs.

(4) 64. Meets with union officials as specified by union contract. ____

(4) 65. Arranges to have parents called or otherwise notified ____
when child is tardy or absent from school.

(4) 66. Evaluates the job performance of custodial, secretarial, ____
and other support staff members.

(1) 67. Confers with other principals and/or district personnel to ____
coordinate educational programs across schools.

(8) 68. Surveys various segments of the school to assess how ____
individuals are perceived.

(4) 69. Attempts to instill pride in school facilities and equipment ____
to control vandalism.

(2) 70. Establishes procedure to use teacher aides and to eval- ____
uate them.

(7) 71. Attends district budgetary meetings and provides needed ____
input.

(8) 72. Keeps informed about new techniques (i.e., in computer ____
technology, human relations) and how they might affect
various staff elements, and encourages appropriate educational effort.

(4) 73. Structures a cafeteria schedule and traffic flow chart. ____

(3) 74. Responds to requests for information or help from var- ____
ious community groups, agencies, etc.

(4) 75. Requests and follows up requests for maintenance, re- ____ pair, and equipment (people and material needed).

(4) 76. Accounts for and monitors expenditure of school funds in ____ accordance with existing laws and regulations.

(3) 77. Oversees and contributes to newsletter for parents and ____ public to keep them informed of school policies and activities.

(2) 78. Provides feedback to custodial, secretarial, and other ____ support staff about job performance.

(1) 79. Defines and implements the objectives and standards for ____ an effective library/media center.

(3) 80. Conducts orientation session for parents; develops spe- ____ cial programs for parents new to the school.

(3) 81. Organizes community advisory groups consisting of par- ____ ents, teachers, and administrators, and meets with them.

(3) 82. Communicates priorities regarding resources and mate- ____ rial to staff, community, and students.

(4) 83. Coordinates with fire department and traffic personnel ____ for smooth operation of school and provisions for emer- gencies.

(2) 84. Solicits substitute teachers and supervises their classes. ____

(3) 85. Works to convince the community to pass bond issues. ____

(4) 86. Provides information to financial auditors on expenditure ____ of school funds.

(1) 87. Encourages the staff to search for and implement new ____ programs.

(2) 88. Encourages teachers to get certified in areas for which ____ expertise is lacking.

(6) 89. Develops and coordinates student activities (athletics, ____ debates, etc.) with other schools in and out of the district.

(5) 90. Finds and develops programs to reduce absenteeism, ____ tardiness, and/or behavioral problems.

(6) 91. Counsels teachers, students, and the staff on personal ____ problems and refers them to appropriate groups.

(6) 92. Meets with leaders of student organizations. ____

(1) 93. Seeks the input of local employers to make vocational ____ programs sensitive to employers' needs.

(5) 94. Explains disciplinary code to students, parents, and the _____ staff in accordance with student bill of rights.

(6) 95. Provides for supervision at student activities. _____

(6) 96. Provides resources and/or training to help the staff rec- _____ ognize and deal with student behavior problems.

(4) 97. Writes faculty handbook to describe school policies, pro- _____ cedures, and attendance.

(1) 98. Monitors and encourages individual student progress. _____

(4) 99. Monitors keeping of records about students (i.e., medical _____ needs, registration, tardiness, absenteeism, etc.).

(5) 100. Elicits staff participation in extracurricular activities. _____

(3) 101. Coordinates and oversees use of school facilities by com- _____ munity groups (i.e., church, recreation, or other purposes).

(2) 102. Involves the current staff in the selection of new staff _____ members.

(3) 103. Ensures appropriate use of community agencies and re- _____ fers students with special needs.

(1) 104. Organizes bilingual curriculum for English-as-a-second- _____ language students.

(4) 105. Requests and pursues district or central resources for _____ maintenance and repair of school plant.

(4) 106. Explains reasons for district-level and federal rules and _____ regulations to staff, students, and community.

(6) 107. Supervises or provides for supervision of bus trips to _____ special events or extracurricular activities.

(1) 108. Reviews use of instructional materials (books, audiovi- _____ sual equipment, etc.) in the school.

(5) 109. Produces student handbook to explain students' rights _____ and responsibilities.

(3) 110. Develops relationships with local media to ensure expo- _____ sure of school activities and needs.

(1) 111. Evaluates curriculum in terms of objectives set by school _____ or district.

(3) 112. Develops communication channels for minorities to voice _____ concerns.

(5) 113. Trains and monitors students to keep them in line with _____ the prescribed traffic and cafeteria flow charts.

(1) 114. Communicates the various roles of resource personnel ＿＿ (nurses, psychologists, curriculum experts, etc.) to the staff and the teachers.

(4) 115. Involves professional and custodial staff members in ＿＿ school maintenance problems that affect them.

(2) 116. Interviews personnel to select people and/or provide in- ＿＿ put into the selection decision.

(8) 117. Participates in professional growth activities: attends ＿＿ professional meetings, reads professional journals, takes classes, or attends seminars on relevant topics.

(1) 118. Encourages involvement of the staff in professional or- ＿＿ ganizations and supports involvement in workshops and classes.

(7) 119. Serves on district-level curriculum and policy commit- ＿＿ tees.

(4) 120. Develops procedures for efficient office routine. ＿＿

(1) 121. Provides for meetings or training sessions in which peo- ＿＿ ple can share ideas they picked up from professional associations.

(2) 122. Observes teachers' classroom performance for the pur- ＿＿ pose of evaluation and/or feedback to teacher.

(4) 123. Develops a comprehensive plan for the orderly improve- ＿＿ ment of school plant, facilities, and equipment.

(3) 124. Provides structure for dialogue and cooperation between ＿＿ faculty and community groups.

(3) 125. Prepares community for educational innovation. ＿＿

(4) 126. Involves staff and/or community in process to refine an- ＿＿ nual budget.

(3) 127. Confers with parents when they visit the school. ＿＿

(6) 128. Attends various student extracurricular events. ＿＿

(4) 129. Constructs a class schedule. ＿＿

(2) 130. Oversees the activities of the guidance counselor. ＿＿

(4) 131. Sets priorities for provisions of materials and resources ＿＿ according to financial limitations.

(5) 132. Evaluates new students to facilitate their integration into ＿＿ the school.

(4) 133. Ensures that fire and tornado drills are carried out and ＿＿ reports their conduct to appropriate authorities.

(4) 134. Supervises ordering, receipt, and distribution of supplies. ____

(3) 135. Attends parent-teacher organization meetings and other- ____ wise supports similar groups.

(5) 136. Establishes orientation activities for incoming students. ____

(7) 137. Confers with district to determine how best to fulfill legal ____ requirements of various programs.

(3) 138. Exercises responsibility for teacher and parent meetings ____ when a parent requests such a meeting.

(4) 139. Monitors the enforcement of various health regulations ____ involving immunizations, health standards in cafeteria, etc.

(6) 140. Supervises the transportation of students. ____

(1) 141. Meets with faculty representatives to discuss faculty ____ problems.

(3) 142. Writes and/or presents reports of school activities to ____ community groups.

(1) 143. Teaches class to serve as a model. ____

(1) 144. Reviews and monitors educational programs to ensure ____ that they meet various students' needs.

(6) 145. Confers with coaches and other activity leaders to ensure ____ space, time, and resource requirements for various activities.

(7) 146. Coordinates testing programs required by the state or ____ otherwise requested of the school.

(3) 147. Establishes procedures and techniques for adequate plant ____ security.

(4) 148. Assesses physical plant and equipment needs in terms of ____ school goals and objectives.

(6) 149. Trains student leaders to be more effective student lead- ____ ers.

(1) 150. Meets with other colleagues to discuss problems, their ____ solutions, and new developments in education.

(6) 151. Plans student assemblies and cultural productions. ____

(1) 152. Coordinates with local vocational education groups for ____ cooperative programs.

(5) 153. Meets with students to explain academic requirements ____ and availability of various programs.

(3) 154. Informs parents of any disciplinary action involving ____ students.

(7) 155. Defends budget needs to Board of Education or district ____ personnel.

(5) 156. Implements program to provide additional instruction to ____ students who do not pass minimal competency tests.

(5) 157. Resolves conflicts in class schedules; works with data ____ processing and teachers to effect solutions.

(6) 158. Authorizes and supervises field trips. ____

(6) 159. Attends banquets or special events to honor outstanding ____ students and/or athletes.

(3) 160. Works with community to develop student activities. ____

Scoring the Zero-Based Job Description Questionnaire

Step 1

On the questionnaire are numbers in parentheses to the left of each task. Count the number of (1)s that you assigned a letter A. If you assigned more than one letter, such as A/B, A/C, or A/B/C, count these right along with those you assigned only an A.

Step 2

Now, turn to the Zero-Based Job Description Score Sheet on page 146. Listed on the score sheet are eight categories that characterize the principal's various tasks. In column N, next to the first category "Educational Program Improvement," record the number of (1)s you counted in step 1 above.

Step 3

Go back through the questionnaire and count the As you recorded next to tasks numbered (2), then (3), and so on through (8). You're counting only tasks labeled A—those you would keep for yourself. Record your tallies on the score sheet in Column N next to the appropriate category.

Step 4

Add and record the total of the numbers in Column N. If you kept all of the tasks for yourself, your total would be 160; if you delegated some of the tasks to others, your total will be less than 160.

Step 5

Next, calculate the percentage of tasks that you kept in each category and record that percentage in Column P just to the right of Column N. The total percentage cannot be greater than 100.

Result/Percentage

Total number of tasks | Number of tasks that you kept
assigned the letter A | in that category (individual
(Total of Column N) | number from Column N)

For example, if you kept 100 tasks for yourself (total in Column N), and you assigned a letter A to 20 tasks in category (1), you would find the percentage as follows:

$$100 \overline{)\,\overset{.20}{20}} \ = 20\%$$

Record each percentage in Column P. Remember, the sum of all the numbers in Column P cannot exceed 100.

Step 6

Now look at page 147, Major Job Dimensions of the School Principal. In this step you will condense the eight categories into four major job dimensions: Educational Program Improvement, Community Relations, Student-Related Services, and Building Management and Operations.

• Add the percentages you recorded on the score sheet in categories 1, 2, and 8 and record that number in Column B on the job dimensions sheet next to "Educational Program Improvements."

• Transfer the percentage in category 3 to Column B next to "Community Relations Activities."

• Add the percentage of categories 5 and 6 and record that number in Column B next to "Student-Related Services and Activities."

• Finally, add the percentages of categories 4 and 7 and record that number in Column B next to Building Management Operations and District Relations.

You have thus codified your ideal role as a school principal into the four major dimensions. The first, Educational Program Improvement, has all those activities that you must do to improve the instructional program of the school. Community Relations Activities include all those tasks that you must do to link the school to parents and the community. Student-Related Services includes all those things you must do to care for students, provide them with activities and counseling services, and handle discipline problems. Building Management Operations and District Relations includes all those tasks that are necessary to keep the building working on a day-to-day basis.

ZERO-BASED JOB DESCRIPTION SCORE SHEET

CATEGORIES	Column N Task Count for Self	Column P Percentage of Time Commitment
1. Educational Program Improvement (the principal's role in academic matters, inservice programs, program evaluation, and curriculum appraisal)	——	—— %
2. Personnel Selection and Evaluation (the principal's role in the selection, improvement, and evaluation of certified and classified staff	——	—— %
3. Community Relations (the principal's role in community activities, communication with parents, and the interpretation of the school to the community)	——	—— %
4. School Management (the principal's role in use and maintenance of facilities, record keeping, relations with the custodial staff, school supplies, and school budget)	——	—— %
5. Student Services (the principal's role in working with counselors, psychologists, student discipline, and student counseling)	——	—— %
6. Supervision of Students (the principal's role in supervising halls, lunchroom, bus loading, playground, student activities and athletic events)	——	—— %
7. District, State, and Federal Coordination (the principal's role in completing district, state, and federal reports; attending meetings; and facilitating communication among these groups)	——	—— %
8. Professional Preparation (the principal's role in professional organizations; reading professional journals; and attending workshops, classes, and other professional growth activities)	——	—— %
TOTAL	——	100%

MAJOR JOB DIMENSIONS OF THE SCHOOL PRINCIPAL

Dimensions of the Principal's Job	Column B How do you think principals *should* spend their time?
Educational Program Improvement Activities (1 + 2 + 8)	——— %
Community Relations Activities (3)	——— %
Student-Related Services and Activities (5 + 6)	——— %
Building Management Operations and District Relations (4 + 7)	——— %

Comparing Your Ideal Role to
How Other Principals Actually Spend Time

Now you have the opportunity to compare your role as school principal as you would like to do it with how the average principal spends the day doing these 160 tasks. You need to transfer the percentages in Column B on page 147 to either Figure A.1, A.2, or A.3, depending on whether you are an elementary, middle/junior high, or high school principal. Record your percentages in the far-right-hand column titled, "Your Ideal Role."

The first two columns of numbers in these figures show the percentage of time that 1,000 average and strong leader principals (all levels) spend on various activities. The third column of numbers represents the same percentage of time spent by principals at the three specific levels. You can compare this with how you actually spend your time. To complete the column "Your Time," you will need to keep a log of your activities using the Time Analysis Record Sheet, on pp. 153–55. Record how you spend time by writing down your activities and the purpose for each of these activities in 15-minute time segments.

Now that you have converted all of your activities to time segments and transformed these time segments into percentages of time that you actually spend in the four larger dimensions of the principal's job, record these percentages in the column entitled "Your Actual Time" on Figure A.1, A.2, or A.3. Some interpretive information for analyzing your data is provided below. For more detailed information, you might want to look at "The Role of the Illinois Principal as Instructional Leader" and "Performing the Role," which may be obtained from the Illinois Principals Association.

Question 1: Which group does your time most resemble—Average, All Strong, or Strong Leader of the same type of school as yours?

Is yours the same as, greater than, or less than these percentages? If yours is most like the category of All Instructional Leaders, congratulations! Chances are you have your job under control. Keep up the good work. If your actual time is more like the Average Principal, you may want to consider developing a personal growth plan that will help you tune your activities to be more consonant with how strong instructional leaders spend their time.

Question 2: How does your actual time compare to the way you think you ideally should spend your time?

If they are different, in what way? Did you spend less time than you think you should in educational programmatic improvement? Did you spend more time with students than you thought you should? If your ideal role looks more like the way instructional leaders spend their time, then you need to think about ways you can focus your discretionary time on instructional matters, rather than routine management functions. If students are eating up your time, there may be some very good reasons for this; start looking at what kinds of student contacts use up the most of your time—discipline problems by any chance? If so, read the section on clinical supervision of teachers in Chapter 2.

Figure A.1. Elementary School Worksheet
How You Spend Your Time Compared to Other Principals

Percentage of Actual Time Spent by You and Three Groups

Job Dimensions of the Principal	Average Principal	Strong Leader Principal	Strong Leader—Elementary	Your Actual Time	Your Ideal Role
Educational Programmatic Improvement	28	41	49		
Community Relations	7	7	8		
Student Related Services and Activities	26	18	20		
Building Management Operations and District Relations	39	34	23		
Total Time Spent	9.5 hrs	10.75 hrs.	10.70 hrs		

Figure A.2. Middle/Junior High School Worksheet
How You Spend Your Time Compared to Other Principals

Percentage of Actual Time Spent Three Groups

Job Dimensions of the Principal	Average Principal	Strong Leader Principal	Strong Leader—Middle/Jr. High	Your Actual Time	Your Ideal Role
Educational Programmatic Improvement	22	41	44		
Community	5	7	7		
Student Related Services and Activities	35	18	22		
Building Management Operations and District Relations	37	34	27		
Total Time Spent	10.0 hrs	10.75 hrs.	10.80 hrs.		

Figure A.3. High School Worksheet
How You Spend Your Time Compared to Other Principals

Percentage of Actual Time Spent by Three Groups and You

Job Dimensions of the Principal	Average Principal	Strong Leader Principal	Strong Leader—High School	Your Actual Time	Your Ideal Role
Educational Programmatic Improvement	25	41	33		
Community	8	7	8		
Student Related Services and Activities	31	18	21		
Building Management Operations and District Relations	42	34	38		
Total Time Spent	10.0 hrs	10.75 hrs.	10.80 hrs		

Time Analysis Record Sheet

On page 154 is a Time Analysis Record Sheet to be used to take a sample of how you actually spend your time. Pick a typical week and log your activities and the purpose for them. Make a log sheet for each day of the week. The sample time record on page 155 is included as a model. Review it carefully. For example, look at the time period 7:30 a.m. to 8:30 a.m.

Note that for each entry both the activity and the purpose are given. If you spend time conferring with a teacher, indicate whether it was about evaluation, supplies, or heat. If you have a telephone call with a parent, explain briefly whether it was regarding a student, a fund raiser, or a teacher. Be sure to complete a record sheet for each day of the week.

After you have kept your logs for an entire week, go back over each one and determine the category for each activity. Read the descriptor for each category on the Zero-Based Job Description Score Sheet, then assign a 1, 2, 3, etc. for each time slot in the small column to the right of each 15-minute time segment.

After you have recorded all of these numbers, go back and count the number of time slots with a 1, 2, 3, etc. (If an activity took less than 15 minutes—say 5 minutes—this would represent 1/3 of a time segment.) Add up the number of time segments that you have coded and record them in Column N on the Actual Time Summary Sheet on page **156**. This sheet is similar to the Zero Based Job Description Score Sheet, and is completed in exactly the same manner. (Refer to page **144** for scoring instructions.)

TIME ANALYSIS RECORD SHEET

Time			Time		
6:30 a.m.	—		2:00	—	
6:45	—		2:15	—	
7:00	—		2:30	—	
7:15	—		2:45	—	
7:30	—		3:00	—	
7:45	—		3:15	—	
8:00	—		3:30	—	
8:15	—		3:45	—	
8:30	—		4:00	—	
8:45	—		4:15	—	
9:00	—		4:30	—	
9:15	—		4:45	—	
9:30	—		5:00	—	
9:45	—		5:15	—	
10:00	—		5:30	—	
10:15	—		5:45	—	
10:30	—		6:00	—	
10:45	—		6:15	—	
11:00	—		6:30	—	
11:15	—		6:45	—	
11:30	—		7:00	—	
11:45	—		7:15	—	
NOON	—		7:30	—	
12:15	—		7:45	—	
12:30	—		8:00	—	
12:45	—		8:15	—	
1:00 P.M.	—		8:30	—	
1:15	—		8:45	—	
1:30	—		9:00	—	
1:45	—		9:15	—	

TIME ANALYSIS RECORD SHEET

6:30 a.m.	2:00 confer w/ 2 teachers re: sched
6:45	2:15 phone call re: student teach.
7:00 paperwork at desk re: letters	2:30 } meet w/ school nurse and
7:15 " re: read memos	2:45 } psychologist re: student
7:30 talk w/ teacher re: heat in room	3:00 } Bus loading
7:45 talk w/ student re: attend.	3:15 } supervision
8:00 confer w/ secretary re: today's tasks	3:30 phone call re: use of building by community
8:15 Halls-supervision	3:45 3 teacher talks: 2 re: supplies 1 re: leave
8:30 paperwork at desk: district	4:00
8:45 questionnaire on bldg. maint.	4:15 District
9:00 } Classroom	4:30 Meeting
9:15 } observation	4:45
9:30 } re: evaluation	5:00 re: SLO's
9:45 }	5:15
10:00 } answer phone calls:	5:30
10:15 } 2 re: students / 1 re: PTA	5:45
10:30 paperwork: memo to staff	6:00
10:45 write summary of morning eval.	6:15
11:00 work w/ sec on purchase orders	6:30
11:15 paperwork: read memos	6:45
11:30 } Lunchroom: supervise	7:00
11:45 } cafeteria and	7:15 }
NOON } eat lunch	7:30 } Return to school
12:15 }	7:45 }
12:30 personal phone calls	8:00 } for
12:45 talk w/ custodian re: lunch-room	8:15 }
1:00 P.M. } post conference with teacher	8:30 } music program
1:15 } evaluated today	8:45 }
1:30 Halls-supervision	9:00 }
1:45 paperwork re: chapter one	9:15 }

ACTUAL TIME SUMMARY SHEET

CATEGORIES	Column N Task Count for Self	Column P Percentage of Time Commitment
1. Educational Program Improvement (the principal's role in academic matters, inservice programs, program evaluation, and curriculum appraisal)	_____	_____ %
2. Personnel Selection and Evaluation (the principal's role in the selection, improvement, and evaluation of certified and classified staff)	_____	_____ %
3. Community Relations (the principal's role in community activities, communication with parents, and the interpretation of the school to the community)	_____	_____ %
4. School Management (the principal's role in use and maintenance of facilities, record keeping, relations with the custodial staff, school supplies, and school budget)	_____	_____ %
5. Student Services (the principal's role in working with counselors, psychologists, student government, student discipline, and student counseling)	_____	_____ %
6. Supervision of Students (the principal's role in supervising halls, lunchroom, bus loading, playground, student activities and athletic events)	_____	_____ %
7. District, State, and Federal Coordination (the principal's role in completing district, state, and federal reports, attending meetings, and facilitating communication among these groups)	_____	_____ %
8. Professional Preparation (the principal's role in professional organizations, reading professional journals, and attending workshops, classes, and other professional growth activities)	_____	_____ %
TOTAL	_____	100%